THE ART OF TEACHING A SECOND LANGUAGE

By
Saeid Atoofi. Ph.D.

Copyright © by Saeid Atoofi 2022
All rights are reserved. No part of this publication may be reproduced, stored in a retrieval system or transmitted in any form or by any means, electronic, mechanical, photocopying, recording or otherwise, without prior permission of the author.

Published by Ingram Spark
Atoofi, Saeid, Ph.D.
      The Art of Teaching a Second Language / Saeid Atoofi. – 1st ed.
Includes index and references

ISBN 978-1-947017-04-7
1. Second Language Instruction 2. Language Education 3. Language Acquisition 4. Teaching a Second Language 5. The Art of Teaching

Cover Design: Saeid Atoofi
Cover image by: Neringa olbutaite, via Pixabay

To my daughter, Sofia

Acknowledgment

It is unwarranted to put a sole author's name on a book. The name implies that the information and knowledge came from the author. But this is hardly the case. No one writes a book alone. Even at its basic level, a book reflects an accumulation of everything someone has learned. But we learned those things from other people. Maybe at most, as authors we can give credit to ourselves of how daring we were to get out to know from as many people as possible. But this is purely theoretical knowledge. All that knowledge was also built on and was supported by a host of institutions and human capital. Additionally, it is a privilege to be a writer. Authors like me are supported and provided by the society as a whole, so we could sit down behind our computers and type-in these words. I thank you all for this opportunity.

In writing this book, I have been particularly blessed to receive support from my family, friends, and colleagues. My wife, Viviana, was a great support and source of encouragement. She provided content and proofreading feedback for some of the chapters on the last-minute notice. Her mom, Sara Drinberg, also very enthusiastically read my chapters and provided meaningful feedback. I cannot thank enough, my dear friend, Sara Behseta, who provided thorough feedback both for the form and the content of this book. Without their help and support, this book would have not been possible.

I am particularly grateful for all the help I received from my colleague, Professor Evelyn Elwell Uyemura. Evelyn read this book in two separate occasions. Each time she provided in-depth and helpful comments to improve the content, proofread the entire book from grammatical and spelling errors, and tightened the discourse so the book would read better. If there are any other errors in the book, they are mine as I added some touch-ups here and there in later stages. With her decades of experience and knowledge in teaching English as a second language, Evelyn's feedback allowed me to reflect on my ideas in this book from the perspective of an expert in the field. Thank you, Evelyn!

Contents

Chapter 1	Introduction	3
Chapter 2	The Art or the Science of Language	11
Chpater 3	What is Language?	23
Chpater 4	How a Child Learns Language	39
Chapter 5	Where: The Journey	46
Chapter 6	Why: Motivation	62
Chapter 7	How: The Method	81
Chapter 8	What: The Content	97
Chapter 9	Who: Learners	113
Chapter 10	Conclusion	126
	Index	135
	References	143

The Art of Teaching a Second Language

Oh, the head!
you are the cause within the cause within the cause

Oh, the body!
you are the wonder within the wonder within the wonder

Oh, the heart!
you are the desire within the desire within the desire

Oh, the soul!
you are the delight within the delight within the delight

Rumi: Rubaiyat, #1742

CHAPTER 1
Introduction

Mercury Lies

We had just finished Sunday lunch in a high-end Peruvian restaurant in Santiago, the capital of Chile. The waiter appeared, and I asked him, "La cuenta, por favor" (the bill, please). In a questioning tone, the waiter responded with only one word, "El Mercurio?" (The Mercury?). I was not sure what he meant to say by using that phrase. By then, I had lived in Chile for about two years, so I knew that the phrase *El Mercurio* had different meanings. In its literal sense, *El Mercurio*, means, either the element mercury, or the planet Mercury. But none of those meanings made any sense in that context. The waiter could not have possibly asked me if I were from the planet Mercury. So, what did he mean? Then, I had an aha moment. He meant the famous Chilean daily newspaper, *El Mercurio*. But I was still confused. Was he offering me a copy of the newspaper? I had to ask for clarity from my Chilean wife. A back-and-forth conversation between my wife, the waiter, and my mother-in-law cleared the confusion. It turns out that the newspaper, *El Mercurio*, has a subscription club that offers discounts to its avid readers dining in upscale restaurants. The waiter was asking me if I had the *El Mercurio* discount, so he could apply it to our bill.

As a language teacher, these simple interactions make me question a lot of taken-for-granted concepts about the nature and structure of language and the way we come to learn and teach it. For instance, in the above exchange in the restaurant, I noticed that, most often, just one word can stand for a whole sentence. The waiter did not even utter a full sentence but just a couple of words with a rising intonation to show that it was a question. The truth is that contrary to a prescriptive view of language, people do not consistently speak in full sentences. For instance, when paying for my food, I can ask a waiter in either a short phrase, such as, "The check, please," or with a less frequently-used full sentence, "Can I have the bill?" But even if I ask in a full sentence, the response will seldom come in full-sentence form. Most probably, the response will be something along the lines of, "Forty dollars." Nobody will say, "Your bill is forty dollars." Even if someone does, it comes across as odd and very formal.

The other thing that I noticed in my interaction with the waiter was that the word *mercury* did not have a meaning. We, as participants in that conversation, gave that word the meaning intended in that context. Words are loaded with our cultural histories and the context they are used in. Let's say, instead of me, it was actually a Spanish speaker from Spain who was dining there in that Chilean restaurant. The Spanish speaker would have been totally clueless as what the waiter had meant by using the Spanish phrase *El Mercurio* (The mercury). If anything, it was actually my less-than-perfect Chilean Spanish that helped me understand part of the intended meaning. In other words, in that context, understanding what *El Mercurio* meant had more to do with me living in Chile than being a Spanish speaker.

But the story of *El Mercurio* does not end here; it gets even better! After that incident, I talked to many Chileans about that interaction. To my surprise, not all Chileans understood what the waiter had meant by using the phrase, *El Mercurio* in a restaurant. It turns out that *El Mercurio* is a newspaper associated with the conservative, right-wing party in Chile. As such, usually individuals from the upper class, or as Chileans call them, *Los Cuicos* (the rich and snobby) read *El Mercurio*. In fact, many of the left-wing and working-class people do not read *El Mercurio*. When the Army General, Augusto Pinochet, overthrew the democratically-elected government of president Salvador Allende in the early 1970 in Chile, *El Mercurio* sided in the favor of the coup. And for that, Chileans have an expression for that newspaper. They say, "El Mercurio miente" (El Mercurio lies). So, in order to understand what the waiter had meant by "El Mercurio?" not only did I have to know Chilean Spanish, but also, I had to be associated with the right-wing in Chile. One single word is so packed with different tones in meaning, culture, nationality, and politics.

Linguists Do Not Lie, But May Not Tell The Whole Truth Either

Other than words that change meaning in different contexts, such as the phrase, *El Mercurio*, natural languages are, of course, systemic and have a structure called grammar. We assume that the grammatical system should be context-free. That is, for instance, we know that the word *good* may have very different meanings in different contexts. What we mean by a "good chair" is very different than what we mean by a "good student" or a "good dentist." However, we assume the present perfect progressive tense in English should have a fixed function regardless of the context it is used in. But in fact, what we call grammar, or the present perfect progressive tense, is only one way of looking at the system of language. In a way, there is no such a thing as "the grammar of English" or "the function of the present perfect progressive" neatly packaged in a certain definition. It is actually those educated in linguistics and its related field, who created grammars. As linguists, we did our best to come up with categories, names for parts of speech, and descriptions and functions for the ways words can or cannot move around in a sentence. The intention was to make it easier to talk about and describe the structure of languages. But I think, deep down, everybody knew that we were just trying to describe something and not what something really is. There is a difference between what red is, and how it is described. Who can ever fully describe a color, an animal, an emotion? But, of course, maybe there is a system to all that. It is just that the description is not the thing itself. I am not sure if we are aware of this discrepancy. I am not sure if we are aware that grammar is only a description for the structure of a language and not the language itself.

Now, as language educators, we are haunted by our own demon. How do we explain to language learners that by describing the grammar of languages, we sought to expand our own understanding of the organization of languages? We really did not intend to teach a second language by teaching its descriptive structure. But now, it is the norm to expect that. The average language learners expect to speak a second language as soon as they know the grammar and sufficient number of words in the new language. But indeed, this is not what happens. So, learners take more language classes because they think that they still do not know enough words and grammatical structures. A lot of honest language teachers and institutions may feed language learners with what they want. They offer them more grammar and more words.

The problem, however, does not go away. It comes back to language teachers and language learners. I have seen it in a countless students. It is really disheartening and demoralizing for anyone to make considerable efforts and not see substantial results. And this is a very common frustration with new language learners. They usually compare their efforts in learning a new language with other types of learning and soon realize that their investment in time and sweat has not been well spent.

Of course, there is nothing wrong with these people; they are actually the norm. In fact, there is seldom, if ever, a person who has become proficient in using a new language – and I emphasize on the word 'using' – with little effort in a short span of time.

Language learners are even more discouraged by their efforts when they watch online videos of so-called polyglots, people who claim to speak 5, 10, or even 20 languages. They appear to speak fluently, switch between languages with ease, and pronounce the words flawlessly. So then, the new language learner may wonder, "Why not me?" Some learners are just starting fresh in a new language and nervous about the task at hand. Some have prior experience in taking many years of foreign language courses in middle or high school. But despite earnest efforts, the mastery in the new language still looks very distant. If anything, the progress seems very slow and cumbersome. Learning a foreign language does not look easy at all.

Sometimes with a lot of effort, language learners try to polish their pronunciation. They even get to advanced levels of foreign language classes, but still fail to handle meaningful conversation in the new language. Some of my students know very advanced grammatical structures in English, such as the future perfect tense that native English speakers are unaware of, or seldom use, such as, "I will have finished my food by the time John arrives". In spite of this ability, those very same learners come to a standstill when you ask them to have a meaningful conversation in English with a native speaker.

Language learners' perception of what they think they need has an impact on their learning process. It is rather impossible to convince our students that regardless of the number of words and grammatical structures they know in English, they will not be able to hold a meaningful conversation in a noisy New York bar with a Yankee fan. Most likely there is nothing wrong with anyone's English there. It is just that some of us think that we know what El Mercurio means until we are paying the bill in a

Peruvian restaurant in Santiago de Chile.

Lecturing Birds on Flying
It's only when the tide goes out that you learn who's been swimming naked.
                                                            - Warren Buffet

Of course, I understand that most of language does not involve knowledge about the real meaning of the word *El Mercurio* when uttered with a rising intonation in a high-end Peruvian restaurant in Santiago de Chile. If anything, this is an extremely rare event. I am aware of that. In fact, most language learners are happy with the basics, just enough to get a taxi in the street, book a hotel room, and have a small chat with their tour guide when visiting a new country. Likewise, most English language learners are less interested in talking with a Yankee fan in a noisy New York bar. But it is the abnormal rather than the normal that gives us the best clue about the inner working of a system or organization. You may draw some unwanted attention if you laugh really hard in a library where everybody is quietly reading books. It is in breaking the rule that makes us aware of the underlying and not-so-obvious rules.

The point is that we often assume that the meaning and functions of grammatical structures are in the words and sentences of a language. However, investigating how native speakers actually use their language, especially in unexpected ways, reveals something very interesting about the organization of language. These events show that the meaning and functions are actually created through interaction rather than any abstract qualities of language itself. In other words, in order to understand what something means, we need to be in the midst of an interaction as it happens. We have to be a relevant participant in the creation of meaning, whether as a speaker, listener, or both. If this is true, how can typical fill-in-the-blank practices of language classes be of any practical use in the acquisition of a new language?

The best-method approach in learning or teaching a new language may in fact exist. However, such approach has to be so general and so wide-ranging that it would not really be the best method for a particular individual. And that is exactly what I try to avoid. If taking a pill such a painkiller can remedy any pain in any parts of the body for any person living anywhere in the planet, regardless of age, gender, and prior and current physiological condition, then it must really work on the lowest biological denominator to have such an effect. But because a pill can remedy any pain for anyone, anywhere, then by definition it cannot be at the same time the best option for every pain and every person. There must be a better option for an individual person. If there is an art in remedying a pain, there must be an art to teaching and learning a second language.

What to Expect from This Book?

This book is primarily intended for language teachers, but it is also readily available for average language learners. I will introduce a new approach to language education, one that views language learning from the speakers' perspective and not the linguists', from what language can be and not what language must be. I have called this approach, *the art of teaching a second language*. I call it the *art* because there is a difference between describing something and knowing how to use it. The former belongs to the realm of academia and the latter to a practitioner who wants to apply knowledge for use. It is one thing to describe and explain the structure of flight in birds and another to see a bird fly. Nassim Taleb[1] calls it, "Lecturing-birds-how-to-fly epiphenomenon." In fact, birds do not know anything about aerodynamics; they just do it. Let us be clear. I am not suggesting that knowledge about the grammar of language does not help us learn the language. Rather, the point is that the abstract knowledge about the structure of a language is only 'a' description of its system; it does not make us speak it and use it. If you want to ride a bicycle, you may get some ideas by reading about cycling, but eventually, you've got to ride a bike. The action of the riding is not solely in the rider or the riding method; rather, riding is a quality that is equally distributed in the rider, the pedals, the history of bicycle, the bicycle, the feet and hands of the rider, and so forth. The mainstream language classroom is geared toward imposing the language into the language learner's brain. For the most part, this language learner is not the rider of language in any sense of the word.

This book consists of ten chapters. After this introductory chapter, the next three chapters provide a theoretical background for a novel approach to language teaching that I have termed *the art of teaching a second language*. I have tried to avoid jargon and complex concepts to make the theory more accessible. In the theoretical parts, I challenge language educators to view language and language learning from a different perspective. I will discuss that, in fact, natural languages are very similar to physical tools like spoons or hammers. Through constant use, a tool, whether a spoon or words, becomes an extension of the body. I will also discuss that our culture-specific experiences are reflected in the languages we speak, and in the same way, whatever language we speak comes to color our experiences.

Chapters 5 through 9 provide strategies and applications for this new theory. I have introduced tools and guidelines that allow language educators to assess motivational factors in their learners, determine a trajectory to language proficiency, and find relevant methods and contents in teaching the new language. Rather than prescribing *the best methods and resources*, I will offer approaches through which language teachers can customize their own language classrooms. I believe this is exactly what sets an artistic approach apart from a prescriptive method usually offered in second language studies. The book concludes with chapter ten that summarizes the main points of this new approach to teaching a second language.

CHAPTER 2
The Art or The Science of Language

El Rut

We are back in Chile again. It was my second day in Santiago. The family went to a supermarket chain called *Jumbo*, for some quick grocery shopping. I was eager to test my primitive Spanish. Back in Los Angeles, where I lived before moving to Chile, I had dedicated every night of the prior two months to studying Spanish. Like a good language learner, I studied Spanish grammar, watched Chilean movies, and every night I added some vocabulary. I thought I had managed to learn enough Spanish to do daily chores. So, I asked my wife to allow me to speak to the cashier at *Jumbo*. To the best of my memory, the following is the actual conversation I had with the cashier.

> Cashier: Buenas dias ("Good day")
> Me: Buenas dias ("Good day")
> Cashier: Acumula punto nectar? ("Do you collect Nectar Points?")

I looked at my wife as I had no idea what the cashier meant by the 'nectar points.' She told me that *Jumbo* customers usually sign up for a loyalty plan to receive points for all their purchases. The plan was called *Nectar Points*.

> Me: No.
> Cashier: Su RUT, por favor ("Your RUT, please")

I did not know what the cashier meant by RUT. I looked at my wife for clues. She told me that RUT is short for El Rol Único Tributario, or the "Individual Tax Number." In Chile, RUT numbers are frequently used to access the databases in places of commerce and governmental agencies.

> Me: No tengo RUT ("I don't have a RUT")
> Cashier: Bueno, como se cancela ("Ok, how do you cancel it.")

Again, I looked at my wife. I knew that *cancelar* means "to cancel," but I did not want to cancel anything. I wanted to pay. My wife told me that in Chilean Spanish, *to cancel* means "to pay."

> Me: Con tarjeta ("with a card")
> Cashier: Con cuota, o sin cuota ("In parts or without parts")

Again, I looked at my wife. I knew that *cuota* means "share," or "parts," but I wasn't sure what the cashier could mean by that. It turns out that in Chile, even for small purchases, you can pay in smaller installments instead of charging your card for the whole amount. Of course, both the credit card company and the vendor receive higher interest for deferred payments. I never knew that one can make deferred payments for very small amounts.

> Me: Sin cuota ("without parts")

> Cashier: Con tarjeta Cencosud? ("With Cencosud Card?")

Again, I looked at my wife for clues. She told me that many retail stores in Chile belong to a bigger conglomerate that has its own credit card company called *Cencosud*. Jumbo supermarket chains prefer and insist that customers pay with that card, as they receive an additional profit when customers use that specific card.

> Me: No, con Visa ("No, with the Visa card").

Then I handed my Visa card to the cashier.

> Cashier: Desea donar cinco pesos a bomberos de Chile ("Do you wish to donate five pesos to firefighters of Chile?")

It turns out that in contrast to the U.S., the job of a firefighter in Chile is an unpaid and voluntary work and it is very common to be asked for donations for firefighters in different places of commerce.

To my astonishment, other than understanding and responding to a 'good day' in the very beginning, I was 100% dependent on my Chilean wife to conduct a very simple and routinized transaction of paying for my grocery. My Spanish had failed me miserably. What had I done wrong? I had experience teaching and learning a second language. If I had trouble learning a new language, how could I be teaching it to others?

The Gravity of Language

As a teacher of English as a second language, or ESL, my students often ask me questions that do not have simple yes or no responses. Most often my students are confused with the article system in English. Is it 'a animal,' an animal', 'the animal,' 'the animals,' or, just 'animals?' Which one is correct, and which one is not? I give them certain rules about the definite and indefinite article system in English, that every singular count noun must have an article, 'an animal' is any animal and 'the animal' is a specific animal. Then they ask me how about "that animal," or "every animal?" Where is the article in these examples? Then I will have to explain that there is another system called *determiners* that also includes the article system. Words like 'that' and 'every' belongs to the determiner system. Then they ask me what about "my animal? Then I will have to explain that even determiners are divided into other categories, such as possessive determiners. But then there are always exceptions to the grammatical rules. Actually, there are lots of exceptions. For instance, I can give them a big list of rules to indicate how we refer to a future action, for instance, by the auxiliary verb *will*, ("You will like the new home."), or the verb *to be going to* ("We are going to take the bus."). But then, rightly they give me many examples where a future action is marked by a present tense ("The class starts tomorrow.").

Frequently, my students are troubled with punctuation rules. They want to become better writers, so they want to know whether we need a comma before a relative pronoun (e.g., what, where, when, who, whom, whose) or not. They ask me, "Teacher, just say it; do we need a comma before 'who'?" They think I am just beating around the bush when I tell them that it depends on many factors, one of which is whether or not the relative pronoun is followed by a non-identifying or an identifying clause. To understand and actually use an identifying clause will take some weeks of instructions and practice. And this is just to point out only one use of the comma.

As language teachers, we know that our learners expect rules in language. They think it will make their lives easier to have a template and apply it to different items. They think that if they know how to create a simple present tense in English, then all they have to do is to plug different English verbs into that system. Language learners also have another misconception about grammar. They think that language is like mathematics or physics. They assume that similar to math, language has equations and formulae. They think grammar is the formula of language. For instance, in mathematics, if we want to calculate the area of a rectangle, we just multiply its width by its length, hence, $A = L * W$. In rule-based knowledge, such as math and physics, we can go from a pattern to individual items. By the same token, we expect items governed by the same rules to produce similar functions and behaviors. The raindrops falling to the ground from the sky behave exactly the same way as the apple that supposedly hit Isaac Newton on the head falling from a tree. Well, both behave the same way because both are governed by the same laws of gravity. Language learners expect language to be the same way. They want to know the rule of a new language and have it fall into their mouth when they need to speak it.

The Arts and Sciences

It does seem odd... that just when physics is moving away from the mechanism, biology and psychology are moving closer to it. If the trend continues...scientists will be regarding living and intelligent beings as mechanical, while they suppose that inanimate matter is too complex and subtle to fit into the limited categories of mechanism
- Physicist David Bohm[1]

In this book, I argue that in contrast to the mechanistic perspective of many natural sciences, language and its acquisition must be perceived as an art. Science tries to come up with universal and objective rules for the way our physical world works by methods of generalization and reductionism. In contrast, the arts strive to understand the unique and subjective experience of an individual about the world. It follows that instead of looking for *general truths* about the world out there, the arts try to find the truth within. Interestingly, an important claim of the arts is that such inner truths are universal, and they can collectively be called *aesthetics.*

In sciences, we look for universal laws governing the natural world, of objective facts that are uninfluenced, untainted, and independent from our human experiences. The laws of motion, from a scientific point of view, is totally independent from our thoughts about it. A rock sliding down a hill will fall the same way it must fall, regardless of what I think or feel about it. And yet the world of living beings seems to be influenced by yet another set of rules, and not necessarily laws, by those of inner subjective experiences. What I feel about how something should be expressed with words may make changes in the way language is used. In fact, this is how for the most part languages have changed; people changed them with use. Although there are always some limiting principles and factors on physical entities, most rules about language can be broken or changed over time. By looking at the history of any language, we are guaranteed to find that it has changed, fundamentally if not completely, within the span of 3000 years. But laws of motion remain constant, not only through time in our planet but probably in the entire known universe.

Another characteristic of science is that it is primarily an object-oriented field. However, art is concerned with patterns. Sciences see the world as things and describe their functions based on their physical properties. From such a perspective, a river is very distinct from a tree. A river and a tree are made of different things and have very different properties and fulfill different functions. From an artistic point of view, a river and tree actually have a lot in common. Usually, both have a big trunk or flow out of which comes out different branches or streams. In arts, we are concerned with similarities in patterns rather than similarities in substances. It follows that physical properties only allow for classifications, categories, and subcategories. But patterns allow for nesting and networking, a feature very dominant in language. We will look at this in more detail in later chapters.

The Art of Teaching a Second Language

The Science Envy

I received a B.A. and an M.A. in psychology before pursuing a Ph.D. degree in applied linguistics and teaching English as a second language. I noticed that like linguists, psychologists also envy mathematicians and physicists. They, too, want to find rules, but this time instead of the natural world, for human behavior. They want to be able to find equations that allow them to plug in data collected from humans and then predict how they will behave. Early 20th-century psychology was dominated by ethologists who studied animal instinctual behavior and reflexes. Their ultimate goal was to deterministically understand and predict animal and human behavior. But soon they found out that there were just too many variables involved in predicating the collective behavior of any organism, especially humans. Psychology as a field responded to this chaotic world with statistics. If there are no fixed laws, maybe certain behaviors occur more frequently given certain conditions. This method has served us somewhat to be able to predict some behavioral aspects of living things, including humans.

But let us not forget that before ethologists such as Konrad Lorenz and Ivan Pavlov, psychology was developed by Sigmund Freud and Carl G. Jung. These men were not interested in applying a pattern of behavior from general to a single case. Quite to the contrary, they were interested in studying a single person. For them, if there was a rule in the way humans interacted with their own kind and environment, it was always to be found from the specific to the general, and not the other way around. In a way, this schism still exists today in many academic fields. There are those who try to extend the physical sciences to the animal and human behavior, to look more 'sciency,' so to speak, and those who believe that the rules of the game are actually made by the very animals and humans, and, as such, tentative, dynamic, and evolving.

I do not think that we should look for a universal

grammar, universal punctuation, or universal pronunciation to explain all structural rules in teaching a second language. I do not believe that such rules exist in language. I think if there is a rule, it is made by us to perform a function, and as such it is best to learn the function first. The grammar of any language is *a posteriori* knowledge. An apple falls because it must fall. However, as speakers of any language, we can choose to play around with words and their structure to create different effects and functions. In fact, this is what it has always been. You will never find an apple that had fallen differently in the past 1000 years or 100,000 years. But look at the history of all languages and you will find languages in constant change, in the way the words and sentences have carried different meanings, sounds, and structures. The same thing is true with every person who becomes our conversational partner. We can never know for sure in what ways someone will use words and language structures to convey certain meaning or functions. We have to listen and hope that we have enough common ground for communication.

To Have Your Apple and Eat It

The structural and law-based approach to human behavior and learning is a Newtonian approach. The Newtonian approach, adopted by the father of modern science, Isaac Newton, perceives of the inanimate world as mechanistic and predictable. The Newtonian approach breaks down the structures and mechanisms into smaller parts in order to explain their function. This approach is heuristic and may serve us very well to explain the laws of motion among physical bodies and the gravitation force between them. However, this system falls short to explain how living beings such as humans, behave and communicate. Human behavior in general, and use of language in particular, is not mechanistic and seldom predictable.

It is unfortunate that some linguists have taken a

mechanistic approach to language education. They have probably done this for two major reasons: first, to appear more "scientific" to the rest of the academic body, and second to offer a clear system to describe human language. If in Newtonian terms, force equals mass times acceleration (F = M * A), then they assumed we should be able to find an equation to show how people form questions in English. Our linguistic law says that speakers place a linking verb before the subject, as in "Are you going to the theater?" In other cases, they use a modal or an auxiliary verb before the subject, such as in, "May I help you?" or "Do you like tea?" to form a question.

But in real life, people may not necessarily follow these prescriptive linguistic rules to talk. And even if they do, it is not because they are trying to abide by the linguistic laws of speaking; people are following certain dynamic conventions to get things done, such a making sure that an expression intended to be a question is understood as a question and not a statement. For instance, in forming a question, other than what the prescriptive grammar tells us, often people just raise their tone at the end of an affirmative statement. For instance, instead of saying "Are you leaving, they may just raise their tone at the end of an affirmative statement, such as "You are leaving?" Or, they may drop the auxiliary altogether: "You leaving?" Sometimes people just add a silence in the middle of their talk, as primary school teachers often do, to show a question, as in, "The elephant is a mammal, and fish is a..." Children fully understand that the silence at the end of that statement is meant as a question. Canadians actually have a unique way to turn something into a question. They just add an 'eh' to the end of every statement, as in, "It's a beautiful day, eh?"

As language teachers, we need to choose our pedagogical style. One style of teaching is based on the conviction that the words in languages are like apples governed by certain laws, similar to laws of gravity. Teach the laws and the words will always fall into the learners' brain and tongue. The second style is based on the idea that the speakers of the language we are teaching chose to have different "fallings" with their "apples." In language, we cannot separate the apple from the falling. Every time we say a word, in an infinitesimal way we have already changed both the apple and the falling. So, instead of teaching the laws of the language, maybe it is best to teach different *fallings* of meanings. Maybe our learners do not talk to be grammatically correct but to be understood correctly.

When we go from form to function, as F=M.A (force equals mass time acceleration), we are in the realm of the law-based world. The law dictates the action and function. But when we go from function to form, we are in the realm of arts. It is the action and the event that produces its own rules of the game. I am under the impression that linguists, yours truly included, have taken the artistic field of language to the domain of law-based world. We can claim it back. We cannot learn or teach a second language by plugging in words into the template of a grammar. Let us start with the type of painting we are interested to create and then figure out what paintbrush and colors are needed.

The Art or the Science of Teaching a Second Language

There is a state of the art in teaching a language, as there is a state of the art in being an architect, a carpenter, a metal worker, or someone who just wants to maintain motorcycle, that is if you have ever heard of Robert Pirsig's[2] famous book, *Zen and the Art of Motorcycle Maintenance*. Other than associating the inanimate world to the sciences and the world of animate to the arts, there is a deep philosophical difference between those who see the world in terms of substances and physical properties and those who see it in terms of function and relationship. The science of architecture is about knowing the laws governing the planning and production of building and other physical structures. The art of architecture is about understanding the differences in functions and patterns in building; how buildings may interact with their environment, and how structures are perceived by our fellow human beings. There is no inherent conflict between these perspectives, but the point of view changes how we pursue something in life.

Most studies in language education are purely derived from scientific perspectives, those that intends to understand the laws associated with the cognitive processing of a new language. The brain is assumed to be a computer that receives language input and must process it in the right way to produce the right output. Frequently, terms used in language acquisition are exactly as those used in computer science as in, "garbage in, garbage out." Mainstream linguistics remains confident that language acquisition is an objective field governed by laws of our nervous system. I beg to differ. Language is our own creation, and we are constantly changing it by the way we perceive of it and use it to do different things. Of course, we do need our nervous system to engage in dance, poetry, cooking, and, of course, learning or teaching a second language. However, it is a misnomer to say that we can know about cooking, dancing, and composing poetry by learning about our nervous system.

Art is about going beyond seeing the world as only a physical substance run by a mechanistic system. Artistic artifacts, such as painting and sculptures are only tangible manifestations that allow us to see something intangible. From a scientific perspective, the beautiful colors we see in a sunset can be explained by a phenomenon called scattering. The rays of the sun setting on the horizon must travel longer in the atmosphere to reach our eyes. The blue color in the light spectrum which we usually see in the sun rays in the high sky is scattered, and only the colors orange, red, and yellow can make it all the way in this long atmospheric journey to reach our eyes. This scientific understanding does not take away my appreciation of a sunset. Our subjective experience of such a beauty, however, is not necessarily dependent on a scientific understanding. I can enjoy the beauty of a sunset with or without a scientific explanation. We love to look at the sun setting on the horizon not because of what a sunset is but mostly because of what it does. Viewing a beautiful sunset can transcend us to reflect on our lives and our place on this planet, or remind us of our childhood, or freeze us in time and space and to forget about our problems, even if it is for a very short period of time.

Similarly, for the most part, the science of language is about what language is, that is, its grammatical structure, the pronunciation system, and its semantic organization. The art of language, however, is about what language does, that is, its pragmatic function and how people use it to do things. Sometimes we need to know the science of language to appreciate its art, and sometimes we do not. Knowing the musical notes is interesting, but will that necessarily respond to Beethoven's symphonies?

The claim in this book is that if we want to teach a new language, it is best to start with what language does rather than what language is. Children never start learning the mother tongue by learning about the parts of speech, such as nouns, verbs, adjectives, and prepositions. They want to do something and find out that people around them use this tool called language to get things done. But more importantly, they may not notice that while they get things done with language, they are doing it in a very particular way which is different from the way other language speakers do. They may not even notice that it is the very same tool that will make them a TikTok generation and not a pen-pal generation. This is exactly what language does. The words, pronunciation system, and the grammatical structure of a language are only devices, tools of musicians or carpenters, if you will, that turn objects into abstract forms. Language allows us to transcend the world. When people learn a new language, they are using somewhat unfamiliar devices of new words and grammar to make sense of the same concrete world they have already known. As language educators, we are here to help them see that for themselves. I call this process, the art of teaching a second language.

CHAPTER 3
What Is Language?

Language As a Tool

> *The specifically human capacity for language enables children to provide for auxiliary tools in the solution of difficult tasks, to overcome impulsive action, to plan a solution to a problem prior to its execution, and to master their own behavior.*
> *- Lev S. Vygotsky[1]*

In its basic form, it is best to think about the human language as a tool, such as a hammer, a knife, a ladder, a bicycle, or a spoon. Of course, human language is more than that; it is more like a semi-living organism, rather than an inanimate artifact or object such as a spoon. But thinking about language as a simple tool is a good-enough metaphor to understand and describe its functions. Thinking about language as a tool also reminds us that tools do not necessarily have to be concrete objects. They can also exist as abstract structures. A computer program, for instance, is not a tangible object, but it is a powerful tool that allows us to perform many other non-tangible or tangible acts, such as balancing our budget in a Microsoft Excel sheet or send selfies across the planet. A human language is also a non-tangible tool that allows us to perform actions in the world, such as asking our kids to brush their teeth, marry a couple by stating, "I now pronounce you husband and wife," or by influencing voters in general elections. In all these instances, language as an abstract structure has been used to perform an actual action in the world.

Similarly, viewing language as a tool allows us to appreciate language for its function rather than its structure. Knowing everything about a tool may not necessarily tell us much about its ultimate and varied functions. For instance, for an alien visiting us from another world, it would be extremely difficult to understand the function of a spoon just by seeing a physical spoon if that alien has never seen a human being, its anatomy, and the way people consume food. An alien needs to see a spoon in action to understand what a spoon does and how it does it. A chisel, a hammer, and a saw combined with raw materials such as nails and plywood will not tell us much about a chair created by a carpenter using these tools and materials. Of course, in hindsight, we can see how the tools and the materials came together to create a chair.

I am afraid we have spent a great deal of time trying to understand the structure of human language as opposed to understanding its functions and, even more importantly, how it achieves those functions. In general, we do not think about language as a tool; we think about it more as an algorithm buried somewhere deep in our brain. In fact, most of language is outside rather than inside of us, and that is what it makes it a tool: a device made by us to do something for us. But through constant use, it becomes extremely difficult to draw a line between where we end, and our tools begin. Again, from the perspective of an alien coming from another galaxy, having isolated knowledge about, let's say, human DNA will not really inform us much about human beings. It is an afterthought to connect the knowledge about DNA to an organism called humans. DNA is just a tool, or a sort of roadmap, to construct organisms. It doesn't make organisms. Additionally, DNA gets its meaning and function in the context of the cells in our bodies. Outside of the cells, it has no meaning nor any meaningful functions. Languages are the same; they are just tools and roadmaps made to perform functions. Words do not have meaning. We bring meaning to words. Without our agreement on the meaning and function of language parts and structures, language is nothing and does nothing.

But as a tool that is somewhat both internal and external to human beings, language allows us reach out and touch more than our fingers can reach. Steve Jobs once made an interesting comparison between bicycles and computers. Jobs stated that in terms of locomotion, we have become the most efficient animal by inventing bicycles. Pedaling a bicycle allows us to get a lot of mileage while spending the least amount of energy in comparison to walking or running, and even flying. He went further to emphasize that computers do the same thing for our minds. That is, a computer is a tool that allows our mind to be very efficient in performing certain mental tasks. Language, as a tool, performs the same way for us. It allows us to do things very efficiently. Language is like an invisible tentacle of our mental faculty extending beyond our articulatory system, reaching distances far beyond our physical reach. It literally allows us to touch other minds without even physically touching a person.

But I think even for Steve Jobs, a computer is still an object, maybe a more complex version of a calculator, which in turn is a more complex version of an abacus. But we must understand that even an abacus is just an extension or a representation of our own fingers, which we use as a tool to do similar mental tasks such as addition or subtraction. For our mind, there is little difference between our fingers and an abacus or a calculator. The mere fact that our fingers are part of our body and a calculator external makes not such a big difference in our perception. Language as a tool works in the same way; whether language is in our brain or totally outside of us is irrelevant to our perception which needs to perform an action in the world using an efficient tool that affords that functionality.

Also emphasizing function rather than structure should remind us that even as a rudimentary object, the function of a tool is not really in the tool. It is not in the tool-user either. We cannot say for instance, that the act of riding is in the bicycle. It is not in the bicycle rider either. In a way, it is between these two. The more these two come into contact and are used together, the more the functionality of riding arises. The function of calculation is not really in our fingers nor in a calculator. Rather, the function of calculation is an emergent quality of the interaction between the mind, fingers, and a calculator. Language is the same. The functionality of language is not really in the structure of the language, such as words, the grammatical structures, or the pronunciation system. It is not in the language speaker either, since a language user must first have access to language. When these two are brought together through use, a functional phenomenon called language-use emerges.

I use the word 'mind' here for the lack of a better word, but I am not really using this word in the Cartesian sense that mind-things are separate from body-things. I highly suspect that even the mind is an emergent quality of our bodies interacting with the world around us. The mind has no agency of its own. It is constantly 'minding.' There is no homunculus in our brain watching the world. Save mystical experiences, the mind is created every second to do mind things. But to this mind, perception is not limited to things with nerve cells in it. As organisms, we are driven to do things such as to eat, procreate, stay clear of danger, show off our new car, etc. And we reach out into the world as much as, or as long as, or as seldom as, or as fast as, or as whatever as we need, with or without specific cells, to get things done. Language is yet another tool created by our collective minds to reach out to the world and to get things done for us. Language is, however, somewhat more intimately and organically connected to us. Our mind perceives of language more like an object with nerve cells like our fingers, rather than a spoon.

Language As a Semi-Living Organism

I think of language as a living thing because as we start to relate to language, whether as a first or second language, the learning both changes us and the language itself. We are in a constant dynamic relationship with language. And this is very much similar to a living thing interacting with its environment. Somewhere I read an interesting example that goes like this. As you are walking down a path, you see an empty soda can. You kick it and most notably it does not kick back. It just rolls around until it stops, obeying the Newtonian laws of motion. Now go ahead and do the same with a neighbor's dog to see what happens. Living things react when you act on them, not in terms of Newtonian laws of motion, but in very peculiar rules of life.

Language behaves the same way. By using languages, we are constantly changing them; language is not a soda can being kicked around. It kicks back. John Haiman, a trained linguist, similarly observed that "the law of gravity is not modified by use: no matter how many times we throw a ball into the air, it will fall to the ground with the same acceleration. The rules of grammar, on the other hand, are modified by use." Language in every aspect, at the level of vocabulary, grammar, and even pronunciation, is constantly changing by use. But this change is reciprocal. Changes in language also change us. Changes in pronunciation make us more American than Australian; changes in vocabulary and grammar make us more of a Twitter or WhatsApp generation than a Myspace generation, the former using shorter phrases, lots of abbreviations, and emojis and memes for expression of ideas and emotions. And all this did not take a 1000 year to change; everything happened in a mere 5 years or so.

Language As Experience

Among several myths that exist in learning a new language, many learners have bought into the idea that language is related to thinking. They assume that since they think using the words in their native language, they must learn how to think with the words of a new language. As language educators, frequently, we hear that new language learners set their goal as "to think in the new language," or sometimes "to dream in the new language." For many, this is the milestone when one is fluent in the second language.

The relationship between language and thinking is very controversial. This discussion usually starts with a theory called *Linguistic Relativity Principle*[2]. In the context of teaching a new language, it is very important to know this theory and understand what is wrong with it. I will try to make it as short as possible, but the theory is relatively complex and philosophical in nature. I will provide support that language is related to our human experiences, part of which translates to thinking. In the context of language instruction, it is very crucial to understand how language relates to experience.

The Linguistic Relatively principle is associated with the work of two scholars, Edward Sapir and Benjamin Lee Whorf, who for the first time began studying less-commonly researched languages, especially those indigenous to North America. While studying Hopi, a Native American language, they were fascinated to find out that Hopi lacked certain expressions and grammatical features we take for granted in English. For instance, they claimed that Hopi lacks any linguistic feature that denotes the flow of time. Although this claim was later refuted, both scholars found enough evidence to propose the idea that people who speak linguistically-distinct languages would perceive the world in fundamentally different ways.

Sapir and Whorf took these arguments as evidence that not only we think within the boundaries of our languages, but that any given language also determines the way we think. In order words, they claimed that, for instance, the lack of temporal continuity in Hopi language determines how the speakers of this language perceive of time, which in their perspective should be very different from the English speakers. This theory entered the mainstream and became very popular, even as mounting evidence refuted a deterministic relationship between the structures of a particular language and the way its speakers think.

Recent accounts of this theory claim that while differences in words and structure of a language may influence our thinking processes, it cannot deterministically shape our reality. That is, a Hopi speaker may experience time in a different way than an English speaker, but the Hopi language does not stop its speaker to experience time in other ways. This conclusion is very intuitive. In fact, you may have never experienced the concept of *sobremesa* as used frequently among Spanish speakers. However, upon explanation, you can understand that *sobremesa* refers to the time one spends with the family and friends around the dinner table, to chat and have a good time. Because this term does not exist in your native language, it does not stop you from understanding the concept.

I arrive at the discussion of language and perception of reality from a different angle, and I hope I can show how this perspective can change the way we attempt to learn or teach a new language. In my viewpoint, the discussion of the relationship between language and thought starts with a wrong foot in the Cartesian philosophy, one that separates mind things from body things. Descartes' famous statement of "I think therefore I am," is the pinnacle of such dualistic perspective that has literally penetrated our every aspect of our modern epistemology (how we come to know), especially in education. In general terms, after Descartes, we think of knowing and learning in terms of a collection of abstract and non-tangible mind-stuff that is different from material things, such as bodies. Of course, language, as an abstract mechanism has been paired with thinking and mind stuff, per

Linguistic Relatively Principle.

    I believe that thinking or any mental activity is not software that runs on hardware called the brain, as usually perceived in neuroscientific literature. I adhere to a recent movement across many fields of study that perceives of bodies as "minded[3]" and minds as "embodied[4]." The basic tenet of such proposal is that through interaction with the environment, living things, including humans, constantly modify, store, and use bodily information about what has worked for them and what has not. Such memory is not necessarily stored in the brain, but all over our cells and even extended into the environment. Within this viewpoint, experience, which is the hallmark of our interaction with our surroundings, is what shapes our behavior, not abstract thoughts.

    So, let us explore a bit the way language, as a tool, can play a role in shaping our experiences. We discussed previously that while most tools may help us interface with the world, the tools themselves do not change in the process. For instance, a spoon has a certain shape and function and retains such properties regardless of how it is used. A hammer, a piano, a car, a knife, or a pen is always what it is. Most people use a hammer to pound nails, but one person may use it to break a glass window. If you don't ruin the hammer in the process, a hammer remains a hammer and the next person will probably use it again to hammer a nail with it. While many tools are able to perform different tasks, they are not changed by use and they retain their original function.

    Languages are not quite like that; language is a tool that affords a wide range of forms and functions. In being such a flexible tool, language is a mediating agent that influences the user, not so much physically, but in the experiential sense. Of course, this is not something new to people who have studied language as an academic field, especially in the applied context, such as in discourse analysis and linguistic anthropology. For instance, language socialization[5] is a research area that investigates how communities use language as a mediating agent to instill social and cultural practices in novices. From such a perspective, children learn their cultural practices mostly through language, and most importantly, they learn language through social and cultural practices. But it is important to know the mechanism and how this is done.

In the Island of the Blind

> *If a lion could speak, we could not understand him.*
> -Ludwig Wittgenstein

In order to understand the relationship between language and experience, I borrow and extend on an example from the wonderful works on *Interactional Expertise,* conducted by Theresa Shilhab[6] and Harry Collins[7]. Let us imagine that one day you wake up and find yourself on an isolated island in which all the people have been blind from birth. Interestingly, everyone speaks your language. However, you quickly notice that while you understand every single word they say, there is something peculiar about their language that does not quite reflect your experiences. For instance, everything they say either lacks visual reference, or it differs from the way you experience the world. Well, this is a no-brainer for you. They are blind, so their language must adapt to the way they perceive the world. They cannot see colors, so there should not be any mention of "a red flower," "the green grass," "a dark cave, or "the shiny spoon," in their language.

But then in the island of the blind you may also notice that even the things that can be expressed only by tactile perception are not exactly articulated the way you experience them. For instance, in a dinner table, you may tell one of the islanders to give you 'the round plate.' The roundness of the plate, of course, can be both seen and sensed by touch. However, you notice that from your perspective, the islanders use more of a flowery language in terms of information about objects as they relate to tactile, auditory, olfactory, and taste information. It is as though their use of language tries to make up for the lack of visual information in other areas of perception. Again, this is not a big deal for you. From a logical standpoint, when you reflect on the issue, you know why this is the case, and you try to live with it. And if you are a linguist, you may even reflect on the idea that for the most part language is interpersonal. We seldom talk to ourselves; we converse; we say something, and our conversational partners listen and continue with what we had just said. A conversation between two or more people is only successful when all parties are willing to collaborate on building on each other's previous utterances. So, a sighted person has to change to the discourse of the blind community if he or she wants to engage in any meaningful conversation.

But as you start living for a longer time on the island, let's say after 20 or 30 years, you may gradually start to change in ways that you had not anticipated before. At this point, it is not only that you have adapted to their way of talking, but also somewhat to the ways they perceive the world. This is not to say that you will not see anymore. Of course, you keep seeing because you are not physiologically blind. But over time, what you see becomes of less and less important to you. You also start to rely more upon your other senses because whatever you say about seeing things become irrelevant to the community you live in.

As you get rid of the visual information from your vocabulary and language, you start experiencing things the way islanders do. You try to locate the monkey on the tree by their howls rather than their motion from one branch to another. You may even find it easier to use your sense of smell to tell a ripe from a green fruit. This is because you are *told* how to function in the world of the blind. To live in the discourse community of blind people, in one way or another, socializes you to rely more on other senses than your visual information. Your change will be very gradual and probably you will not even notice it yourself. You would only notice it if another sighted person arrives at the island and tells you that you talk and behave like a blind person.

Now, things get even more interesting when you bear a sighted child on the island. There is a very good chance that a sighted child born into a blind community would come to experience the world in pretty much the same way of a blind person, or very close to it, merely by exposure to the discourse of the community of the blind. This may seem very farfetched, but as I give you more examples from different experiences, you will come to notice that this is actually what is happening to you and your language right now.

Well, let us reverse the condition now. That is, now imagine that you are a blind person coming from the society of blind people and reach an isolated island where everyone is sighted. Of course, their language is rich in visual information, which means nothing to you. But you start communicating with them in your common language. Over time, you come to realize that all the visual information is somehow related and has a pattern. The words may not make sense to you, but the overall use of language comes to enrich your experiences in a different way that you had not imagined before. Over years of living in the sighted community, you come to talk about the world in a different way, than let's say another blind person who just arrived from the blind world to the island of sighted people. While you still cannot see things, when you talk about the world, your language is rich in descriptive words that appear to have the experience of a sighted person.

This may come as a shock to you, but in a way, all of us are blind people arriving on an island of sighted people or vice versa when we learn a new language. My community is not literally blind, but it is involved in certain routines and practices that are somewhat different from another community that, for them, might feel like missing a sense. My language reflects such practices and experiences. The differences are not really about the new language with new words and new grammatical structures but more about how the experiences are translated using words and grammar. If anything, the words and grammar only show how those experiences are collectively felt, shared, and expanded on.

Of course, as human beings, we share a lot of experiences. There is a great overlap of mutual emotions, ideas, dreams, and concepts between cultures and communities. But going from one language to another is an adjustment from the collective experiences of one culture and community to another using language. Language becomes a medium, a tool, to transfer experiences and in return becomes pregnant with those experiences. The relationship between experience and language is not one-way, only from experience to language. In fact, as demonstrated in the example of the blind person living among sighted people, language also influences how we experience things. Such relationship recursively builds on both language and experience.

Similar recursive experiences also happen with people and the use of tools. Construction workers who have used their tools to build homes need relearning how to use a similar tool to build furniture. It is not about the differences in tools – although there might be some – but the important part is about doing different things with the tools. Both may be driving a nail into a piece of wood, but there are differences between a cabinet-maker's hammer and that of the construction worker. The way tools are held and used also changes because every profession does something different with a seemingly-similar tool. In a sense, when we learn a new language, this is what we do. More than learning words and grammatical structures, we relearn how our words and the systemic aspect of our language differ from another language speakers, and what these aspects enable us to do.

But it is important to point out that when we say that language is a reflection of cultural differences, we are not necessarily talking about culture in a broad sense as understood by a layperson. Culture does not necessarily mean Western culture versus Eastern culture, or Greek culture versus German culture – although such differences leave their marks on languages as well. Nations are not the only category that binds people into a similar culture. In fact, there are many nations in the world with different ethnicities who share similar cultures, some of which even speak different languages. Iran, for instance, is composed of many different ethnicities, such as Turks, Kurds, Balochis, Gilakis, and many more. Despite fundamental differences in language families, learning Azeri Turkish for a Persian speaker is a lot easier than for an English speaker because they share very similar experiences and cultural values. The reason is that while an Azeri and a Persian speaker may be using different languages, they are trying to achieve many similar functions and experiences.

Conversely, there are many people who seem to speak the same language, but often have a communication problem due to the lack of shared experiences. Imagine an average English speaker who just enters an international conference room with participants discussing subatomic particles, all in English. That person will most likely fail to understand most of the conversation. While there might be some technical words used in the conference that an average person does not know, in general, the problem is not lack of knowing the jargon terminology. Even knowing the meaning of all the words, a person still will not be able to follow the discussion or engage in the conversation. The problem is not English; it is the lack of shared knowledge and experiences. However, many of the same participants who come from different countries and may struggle with their English skills will have no problem in understanding the ideas and even engaging in the discussion.

Language as Identity

One time in Chile, I was standing in a checkout line in a supermarket called *Lider*. It was close to the 18th of September, the Chilean National Day. During this time, it is customary that people fly small and colorful kites as part of the celebration. There were lots of kites on display for sale hanging from the ceiling of the supermarket. A young boy, probably around 7 years old and his mom were in front of me in the line. The boy saw the kites and joyfully screamed, "Mama, Mama, cometa, cometa" (Mommy, Mommy, kites, kites). The mother got really upset and screamed back at the child, "Hijo, volantin, no cometa" (Son, kites, no kites). *Volantin* is the Chilean Spanish for the more generic word, *cometa*, meaning "kite" in English. I imagine that the child must have seen a lot of cartoons dubbed for more general Spanish speakers, and he came to use the word *cometa* instead of *volantin*.

But why would a Chilean mother have to be upset that her child is using a non-Chilean Spanish word, for an object, a kite? What is the big deal, you may ask? The mother had enough reasons to be upset about the incident. In her world, Spanish is not only a medium of communication. If this was the case, the communication was successful. The child used a word that the mother understood. But the instance of the Chilean mother to use only Chilean-specific words shows that language is more than communication; to a great extent, specific use of language shows who we are, in this case, a Chilean Spanish speaker and not an Argentinian Spanish speaker. This, however, is not unique to a Spanish speaker. The Southerners in the U.S. are also proud to use their Southern accents and their word *y'all*.

Eight Words for Cousin

In Iran, where Persian is spoken as the national language, there is no single word for *cousin*. There are actually eight distinct words for different types of cousins. Similar to many countries in the Near East, such as in Iran, the extended family plays a pivotal role in daily activities. As such, being a cousin to someone is an important familial relationship. To just say, "yesterday I talked to my cousin on the phone," in Persian, can create a lot of confusion for people. For instance, they would be baffled as to whether it was a male cousin or a female cousin, the daughter or son of your aunt or uncle, or the son or daughter of your aunt from the mother side or your father side. And that is exactly how the word *cousin* is distinguished in Persian, in eight distinct words.

The Persian language reflects such differences because it needs it. There is a possibility of romantic relationship between *dokhtar amoo* (the daughter of the uncle from the father side) and *pesar amoo* (the son of the uncle from the father side) when both have similar age. Two *dokhtar khalehs* (the daughters of aunts from the mother side) usually have a very close, almost sister-like relationship. The reason is that their mothers are also sisters and they frequently get together and meet at each other's homes. Such a relationship usually is not as strong between two *dokhtar daees* (the daughters of uncles from the father side). So, in learning Persian, learners are not learning the word *cousin*, they are actually experiencing and identifying with what it means to be a cousin in Iran. Many other words and grammatical structures in Persian are similarly related to cultural and historical experiences.

Of course, this is not limited to Persian; every language has its own way to reflect experience and identity, in words, in grammatical structures, in pronunciation, in discourse, and even in being silent and not saying a word. In contrast to many Latin American cultures where people constantly talk over one another, in Japan, for instance, people do not overlap while someone is talking. One must talk as briefly as possible and give time to his or her interlocutor to speak. As a listener switching to be the next speaker, one also must keep silent for some seconds making sure that the previous speaker is done talking. In this example, not talking is actually talking. It is communicating a culture-specific style of communication.

In this chapter, we discussed why it is important to consider language as a living tool rather than an algorithm buried in our brain. Furthermore, it was argued that language reflects our shared experiences, and such experiences recursively enrich and expand on the language we collectively use. Finally, we examined the role of language as a tool that creates identities for communi ties of people. The next chapter discusses the process of language acquisition in children and contrasts that with those of adults.

CHAPTER 4
How a Child Learns Language?

Banging the Words Around

> There is a parallel confusion in the teaching of language that has never been straightened out. Professional linguists nowadays may know what's what, but children in school are still taught nonsense. They are told that a "noun" is the "name of a person, place, or thing," that a "verb" is "an action word," and so on. That is, they are taught at a tender age that the way to define something is by what it supposedly is in itself, not by its relation to other things. Children could be told that a noun is a word having a certain relationship to a predicate. A verb has a certain relation to a noun, its subject. And so on. Relationship could be used as basis for definition, and any child could then see that there is something wrong with the sentence "Go is a verb."
> - Gregory Bateson[1]

To understand how we acquire language, let us go back again and view language as a simple tool. I think even for professional linguists this is still a very farfetched idea. Think about a child for the first time is given a spoon. She might start to see the spoon first as something to grab in her fist, then bang around on other nearby objects, then put it in her mouth, and finally use it as intended to intake food. This process, of course, will take some time; it is gradual, needs a lot of practice, and more importantly, involves lots of hits and misses until the child is able to use a spoon as a spoon. Although at the physical level, neither the child nor the spoon changes, when these two interact with one another, in a sense, both the child and the spoon keep changing property, function, and utility through this coming-togetherness.

The use of the spoon would have gone very differently if, let's say, a cat was confronted with a spoon. Of course, the cat also goes through a sort of experimenting with a spoon, but our human interaction with objects, especially those made by us and for us, is very distinct from that of other animals. This is not to say that cats are not smart, but they are never going to pick up a spoon and use it to eat! A spoon and the way we use it actually says a lot about us. A spoon is not a random object that we happen to use for eating. The handle is made for our easy grip. The scoop at the end is also crafted in such a way that it can pick up a certain quantity of food and deliver it efficiently to the human mouth. In short, a spoon is made for our fingers, to scoop our food, and deliver it to our mouth.

We also need to bear in mind that our tools, such as a spoon, have gone through a lot of evolution through time, both in terms of the form and function. And they will keep changing more to be consistent with our future foods and changes in our cultural style, taste, and ecology. When a child starts banging a spoon around, she is not merely just learning how to handle an object; she is interacting with an object with a long history behind it. This notion does not immediately come into our conscious attention when interacting with human objects. Yet by using the spoon, the child is basking in the glory of all that history. That history is the accumulation of our interactions with a type of tool which we collectively call a spoon. Similarly, in learning a language, we are basking in the glory of a long history of hits and misses and experiments with a tool called language.

If we stretch the argument a bit, handling a spoon is actually somewhat similar to the way that a newborn infant learns to use her fingers. Watch an infant trying to use her limbs during the first months of birth and soon you realize that knowing how to use our fingers and toes is for the most part a learned behavior that comes through a lot of practice. The only difference is that our fingers are attached to our bodies and our nervous system. A human tool, such as a spoon, however, is not anatomically attached to us. That, of course, matters and we will discuss how it matters. But, just for having a point of comparison, watch a professional butcher handling a knife and you'll notice that skilled butchers handle a knife almost as an extension of their body, as if it were part of the nervous system.

Language as an Extra Limb

One way to think about language acquisition is to perceive it as a knife of a butcher or a spoon in the hands of an adult. These tools do not have to be anatomical limbs attached to our body; with practice, we can become so proficient in using them that at one point it really does not matter if they are attached to our body or not. For our perceptive and cognitive apparatus, it is almost indistinguishable where the hands end, and the spoon starts. In fact, as we scoop up the food, it seems as though it is our fingers that are reaching out to the food. When we become proficient language users, it feels the same way. By extension, words become part of us or at least can be perceived as an indistinguishable and inseparable part of an ecological system.

I greatly admire Gregory Bateson, an English anthropologist and cyberneticist, whose wonderful work on *Systems Theory*[2] advanced many fields, especially education. Bateson had a unique approach to the way we come to learn. In one of his books,

Bateson[3] wonders where is the 'I' or the perception, in a blind man who is walking along a sidewalk using his cane: tap, tap, tap. He asks whether the 'I' is in the brain, the hand, the cane, or the sidewalk. It is apparent that all these are parts of what the blind man is using to perform the action of walking. For Bateson, the act of perceiving the world for a particular function, in this case, called 'a blind man walking,' is as much in his brain as it is in his fingers, cane, and even the sidewalk. Yes, it is also in the sidewalk. A sidewalk is not an arbitrary pattern in the ground. The blind man uses the knowledge of a specific structure called the sidewalk to navigate his or her surroundings.

Learning What Is in the Middle

By reducing the responsibility of brain in perception and learning and spreading it to other parts of the body and objects in our environment, we have not yet addressed the question of where and how perception and learning occurs. We just came up with more responsible parts. But this is not what Bateson intended to convey with his example. He wanted to make another major claim, less discussed in cognitive and neuroscience. The point is that perception really is not inside things but between things, or rather within the borders they meet. In his example then, the perception of navigation is at the borders where the fingers meet the cane and the cane meets the sidewalk. It is the system that perceives, not any one of the things.

Similarly, for French philosopher, Gilles Deleuze[4], learning a language is like learning to swim or to surf. It is a wonderful metaphor at many levels. First, it may seem that our body is riding the surfboard. This is not true. If anything, we are riding the waves using the surfboard. Of course, the surfboard is a specific tool to ride on waves. But the board is used to do something else: to coordinate between three moving surfaces: the waves, the board, and our feet. Very similar to the previous example, the hand, the cane, and the sidewalk are all part of one function: to walk. In the case of surfing, it is also ridiculous to assume that learning to surf is in the surfboard or in the brain of the surfer or his or her legs or feet. The learning itself happens between the feet of the surfer touching the surfboard, and the surfboard touching the water. All in these between-places must become coordinated for learning to happen.

Learning a language happens in the similar way. When we are learning a language, we are not learning about the language; we are learning how to use this tool called language – which in the previous examples was a cane or a surfboard – to perform language acts, that is to accomplish something with language. Like surfing, in using language, there are a lot of misses and hits, lots of falling and getting up, lots of fine-tuning to do proper acts in different places, in different contexts, using different media, and sometimes for different audiences. It is not one-size-fits-all as we sometimes teach in language classes with those tidy fill-in-the-blank exercises. We can start practicing how we should stand on a surfboard on the sand, and this is actually how novice surfers start. But eventually, the learning happens when we are in the water, clashing with the waves, when our feet touch the surfboard touching the waves. The same process happens when we speak. Our minds and tongues must touch the words, touching the people's mind. The meaning of what we say is in-betweens, not in the tongue, not in our brain, not in the words alone.

But what does it take for these in-between surfaces to become coordinated? When we see an infant banging around a spoon, the acquisition of learning on how to handle a spoon seems random. It seems like there is an 'aha' moment for the child; she gets it. This is because our eyes are trained to pay attention to the movement of the spoon. But for the child, the one who is experiencing it, something else is happening. The child is not really learning how to handle a spoon; rather, she is acquiring the relationships between patterns; how certain actions can predict certain outcomes, and what is similar or different between them.

The child finds that using a spoon to eat mashed potatoes is not the same as using it to eat peas, or Jell-O. But this is far from Pavlovian conditioning. Every iteration, every seemingly repeated action is a bit different from the previous one. It can't be conditioning. Conditioning must be the exact same repetition. The child is not even learning the relationship between physical things; she is learning the relationship between patterns. Such learning is not concrete, but metaphoric.

As human beings, our learning first starts with direct observation and experience with the natural world. However, later language, to a great extent, expands on our perception about the world. First, language turns objects into concepts. We do not need to see or point to a book in order to talk about a book. A book can exist as a concept in our minds, and we can engage in a lengthy conversation about the shape, content, genre, and type of book without ever seeing it. After seeing numerous types of books, *book* is not a thing anymore; it becomes a concept.

Second, language, as a conceptual tool, also allows us to collectively share experiences, without direct individual experiences. Almost nobody, including physicists, have ever personally experienced a black hole. But we can still understand the concept of a black hole, as a real physical thing, by being involved in the discourse of a community of humans called physicists.

I will make an unusual claim: a child does not learn a language; a child learns how to become a functional human in a community of humanity using a human tool called language. In other words, for children, the intention is never to learn language. They just realize that most things they need to do requires a tool called human language. Furthermore, they recognize that this tool does not necessarily point to concrete objects; most often, the words and the system that puts the words together, which we call grammar, index shared concepts and experiences in their community.

Adult language learners by contrast, have already mapped out many of the necessary human concepts and internalized a lot of humanity's shared experiences. As language educators, we should be aware that adult language learners may appear like a child who is learning a new language; however, they are leaps and bounds ahead of a child who is just learning to utter her first words and sentences. We will discuss this in more detail in the next chapter.

CHAPTER 5
Where: The Journey

Ford vs. Picasso

> ... *To be an artist means: neither to guess nor to count: to mature like a tree, which doesn't hasten its growth and stands assertively in the storms of spring without the fear that the next summer may not come. It will come. But it will only come to those who are patient and are willing to wait for it as if the whole eternity lay before them, so carefree quiet in far away. I learn it every day, I learn it with pain, to which I am grateful: patient is everything!*
> – Rainer Maria Rilke, Letters to a Young Poet

Art has no beginning or end. A child dribbling lines that somewhat resemble a cat on a piece of paper may not recognize her work as a masterpiece, but she does understand that the lines were intended to express an artistic form, and she is happy with that. In contrast, a car, as a manufactured product, a technological artifact, at least from an engineering perspective, has a very definite beginning and a very definite end. There are no in between states. It is either a car or not. A piece of art intended as an art is almost always art. A car is only a product when it is finished as a car.

As language educators we might have given the wrong impression to our learners that learning a new language is similar to manufacturing a car. They imagine that they have to be adding pieces to their new language learning until is a whole language. As such they expect a beginning and an end to that manufacturing process. But language learning is indeed a journey, and in every step, language learners are painting their path towards speaking the new language, always progressing and always using their own creation.

As language teachers we are often asked how long it takes to master a new language. There is a whole industry promoting the assumption that, using the right method, you can master a language in a specific amount of time. There are language programs, institutions, books, interactive CDs, and apps that claim to teach a new language, any language, to anyone, in a year, 6 months, or even as little as 3 months. There is a hidden message in these marketing strategies. The language learners wrongly assume that they become fluent in a language in a certain amount of time. It is as though there is an on-off switch that turns on after a set amount of time and then, voila! they are speaking the new language. So, a new language speaker may think, "Oh, I only need to live in Spain for one year and then I'll speak Spanish," or, "I will take introductory, intermediate, and advanced Chinese and then I'll speak Chinese." What could be beyond advanced Chinese?! Right? Of course, the last statement is meant to be sarcastic!

The language education industry has set up the learners for unreasonable and unattainable goals. Language learners will be hugely disappointed when they do not see themselves anywhere close to mastering the new language after three months, six months, one year, or even three years. And taking all the grammar courses in Chinese will not make one speak Chinese. Language learners may never realize that there was something wrong with the promise they were given; they may think that there is something wrong with them, that they were incapable of learning a new language. But, of course, this is not the case. If there is anything wrong, it is with those promises and not the language learners.

Learning a new language is a journey. It is an interactive and dynamic process that involves many parts. For the most part and for most of us, what we consider complete fluency, will take quite some time. Yes, there are some milestones here and there, but overall it is a journey with no beginning and no end. It is better to give our language learners a more realistic stance toward their language learning growth and goals than the fantasy of being fluent in a new language in three months. It has never happened, and it will never happen.

Not a Child

One mistakes adult language learners commonly make is to compare their progress with that of a child learning the mother tongue. For many reasons this is an unjustified and unwarranted comparison. To an untrained eye, it appears that a child learns a language, or even two or three, in a very short amount of time. For instance, for adult language learners, correct pronunciation of the new language, or as it is commonly but mistakenly referred to, *accent*, is one of the most evident and more difficult features of proficiency in the new language. In contrast, for a child, correct pronunciation is seldom an issue. Hence, adult language learners arrive to the conclusion that children have a very special ability in learning a new language, forever inaccessible to them.

It is true that there are some aspects of language that are acquired in early childhood, but the proficiency of an adult language user is in no way comparable to that of a native speaker child. The depth and breadth of language used as an adult, whether as a first or second language, by far surpasses anything a

4-year-old child could even dream of. Yes, the articulation of sounds is cemented in early childhood and become increasingly difficult to attain in adulthood. And yes, a native speaker child has an intuition about the correct order of words, something that an adult language learner must compensate with learning grammatical structures of the new language. But the advantages of a child over an adult language learner for the most part stops right there. In fact, an adult language learner is in a far better place in learning a language than a child. In the following, I attempt to show why adult language learners are in more advantageous place.

Walking Parallel Paths

In order to appreciate the way adults learn new things, especially new languages, we need to abandon the mainstream mechanistic theories of education that assumes learning happens linearly and additively. An artistic perspective recognizes that learning happens through recognition of connections and patterns. The way we intellectually analyze the world can be quite different from the way the world actually functions. For instance, we think about the living world and its behavior from a very physical and mechanical perspective. It is as though the world is constructed through adding material things together in order to create organisms and that the behavior of organisms can be abstracted through their physical substances.

Artists often see the world the way the world sees itself, through patterns rather than through substances. Gregory Bateson[1] noted that it was first Goethe who observed,

> That if you examine a cabbage and an oak tree, two rather different sorts of organism, but still both flowering plants, you would find that the way to talk about how they are put together is different from the way most people naturally talk... we talk about "things," notably leaves or stems, and we try to determine what is what. Now Goethe discovered

that a 'leaf' is defined as that which grows on a stem and has a bud in its angle; what then comes out of that angle (out of that bud) is again a stem. The correct units of description are not of leaf and stem but the relations between them. These correspondences allow you to look at another flowering plant- a potato, for instance and recognize that the part that you eat in fact corresponds to a stem.

Whether we think that a cabbage and an oak tree are just different substances rather than parallel forms of being may not cost us a lot. We have many wrong assumptions about everything, some get corrected over time and some just becomes habits of thinking. However, learning and teaching in a wrong way is not something we should consider as a good habit of thinking or acquiring and transferring new knowledge.

Our lifelong learning as adults significantly influences all other types of learnings, including learning a new language. Let's say, if you have been playing the guitar for many, many years and now want to learn the piano, you are far ahead of a person who has not played any musical instruments at all. In fact, for a while, you may play the piano with a guitar *accent*, but that does not bother you a bit. Similarly, if you have been drawing portraits for many years and now want to learn still life painting, you are far more ahead of someone who has never painted at all. In fact, you may draw your still life with a portrait *accent*, too. The same can be stated for someone who has worked on fixing cars and now wants to take on fixing trains, or a marathon runner who now wants to learn water polo. In all these cases, the skill may seem to be quite different, but there is a whole lot of hidden learning that can be readily transferred from one field to others if we think about the world not in terms of things but patterns and relations.

Concepts, Not Words

Imagine a typical toddler playing around with her dad. All of a sudden, she sees, for the first time in her life, a cat passing by.

The curious toddler looks back and forth between her dad and the cat, until the dad saves the day by uttering, "Cat, cat." Our intelligent toddler understands that there must be a relationship between the utterance of the word "cat" and the animal which just passed by. So, she also repeats, "cat, cat." The dad, of course, repeats, "Yes, cat" to reinforce the learning. Interestingly, some days later, the dad and daughter are in the park playing again and here comes a neighbor with a dog. Our toddler joyfully showcasing her expertise in language points to the dog while looking at her dad and says, "Cat." The dad is, of course, amused. So, he responds back, "No, dog, dog." For the involved dad, the situation is really confusing. The toddler, however, is very clear why she called a dog a cat. But upon hearing the dad's response, now the toddler has to do some readjustments. She might think to herself, "I thought everything furry and walking on four legs is called a 'cat.'" Or, she might think to herself, "Maybe 'cat' is that particular thing – as we use for proper nouns, for instance – in a way my dad is also called 'Steve.'" And then, after seeing and hearing more cats and dogs, finally our toddler will *understand* that first, *cat* is a category of things and not a proper noun and, second, there are categories inside other categories, as there are category of things that are called animals, within which are other categories, such as dogs and cats, and even more categories within each one that are called, poodle and German Shepard dogs, and Siamese and Persian cats, respectively.

As adults, we have already mapped out the world of meaning, the categories, the subcategories, and the relationship between them. However, this is not true for a child. Children are not learning a language; they are learning the world through language. For adults, the word *table* does not refer to a particular object; it is a concept. And that is why as adults we do not need to see all the tables in the world to call a particular one a table; we know that anything with a horizontal surface, certain number of legs, made from almost any hard material, and manufactured to function for eating, working, or holding up objects, can be called a *table*. Adults understand *tableness*, rather than *table*. But a child must understand, sometimes literary one by one, that all objects and ideas are not things but concepts. In fact, a table is not a thing; it is a concept.

It may not appear as such, but as an adult, we are far ahead of a child learning the mother tongue. Nobody will ask a two-year old to fill-in a loan application, contact the department of motor vehicle to set up an appointment, or settle an argument with a coworker. We do not expect that our children listen to CNN and understand political debates. For that, first they need to understand Wall Street, the judicial system, political reform, the Cold War, presidential veto, first amendment, tax return, refugee crisis, climate change, ban on high-capacity magazine, Brexit, Libertarian Party, LBGTQ, United Nations, debt relief, the Federal government, grand jury, trade deals, House of Representative, decriminalization of marijuana ... and a thousand other words and phrases. But these are not just words that that a child needs to understand. These are all concepts, and more importantly, they are all tightly related concepts, frequently one leading to another, all with their histories and each with different shades of meaning in a given context. There is no way a person can only learn about the meaning of *decriminalization of marijuana* by itself without knowing anything about other concepts, such as laws, drugs, legislation, controlled substances act, prohibition, advocacy, medical benefits, organized crime, Drug Enforcement Administration, and many, many other words and concepts.

A child's journey to learning a language is very different than that of an adult trying to learn a second language. Over time, a child must come to understand the relationship between words and how they index concepts. Most adults have already conceptualized the world through words and have an extensive understanding of the relationship between them. For an adult, learning words in the new language is often a translation from one language to another. The real challenge for an adult language learner is turning the knowledge about the new language into the skill of using it, from knowing the musical notes to playing the piano.

Mapping the Journey

Thus far, this chapter has tried to show that the path to learning a new language has certain characteristics that a novice learner might not initially expect. First, contrary to what the average language learner may believe, gaining a real-world, full competency, in a new language is a long journey, seldom, if ever, achieved in months, and, for majority of learners, not even in years. Second, competency in a new language is not an end to a long journey. Everywhere during this journey, a language learner will be using the language functionally despite seemingly insufficient vocabulary or grammatical knowledge. And third, even a novice second language learner is leaps and bounds ahead of a 2- or 3-year-old native language speaker in understanding and interacting with the complexity of real-life situations.

While the North Star will always lead us to the geographical north, a new language learner, however, needs to have a compass for navigating the terrain of reaching competency in a new language. The following is a guideline to help language learners to create that compass and to map the terrain of learning a second language.

To Plan or Not to plan

Most aspects of modern life, from the simplest to the most elaborate, are planned out, from the beginning to the end. Even planning for a night out, such as eating out in a nice restaurant requires reservation, sometimes days in advance, and that not only must include the exact day, but also the exact hour and the exact number of guests. Pursuing a bachelor's degree in any academic field follows a very precise and complete curriculum, from the beginning to the end of the program, which includes the number of classes, required units, and maximum duration of the program. Even seemingly unplanned aspects of an academic degree, such as the possibility of picking elective courses, choosing or changing a minor degree, and alternative routes to certification, are all well-regulated in advance.

There is a tendency to think about acquiring a new language in the same framework of getting a degree, that there must be an exact roadmap with a precise beginning and an end. But there is not. Ask people who have taken Spanish 1, 2, and 3 in college. They are not typically fluent speakers of Spanish. Spanish 1, 2, and 3 is not the roadmap to learning Spanish, nor is basic, intermediate, and advanced Japanese a roadmap to learning Japanese. These are conventions invented by curriculum designers to persuade the dean of the language department that as teachers we can measure learning in grammar, vocabulary, and pronunciation in a foreign language. In a typical college class, a foreign language teacher spends two hours teaching a new tense in the target language. Such teaching is usually followed by individual or group practices, such as fill-in-the-blanks and grammar quizzes. These discrete bites of language are easy to teach, and they are easy to test. Whether the language learner will get something from that lesson is secondary to most language institutions. Of course, some proficiency comes from it, but that is not actually the intended goal. The goal is to make the learner (and the dean of the language department) happy by delivering a measurable product. For most language-teaching organizations, the map to learning a language looks very concrete and very well-planned, but the target is not to speak and use the new language; the target is to break down the language into simpler components that can be individually learned and assembled together, like parts of a car.

Rerouting Your GPS from Paris to Dushanbeh

The journey to learning a new language is not on a direct path, from point A to Z with constant velocity. It involves constant turns, change of speed, and trying out different roads. Well, it may not be as chaotic as trying to find a shipping lane to India from Spain to buy spices and ending up in the Americas, as Christopher Columbus did. It is more like setting one's GPS to go from Paris in France to Dushanbe in Tajikistan. Depending on the number of cars on the road, accidents, road conditions, and most importantly, and what the driver decides to do on the way, the GPS will keep rerouting to get there. While the destination is clear, many factors will influence the way the driver might change routes, speed up, slow down, or stop for some time. Even if the destination is not achieved, the driver still has seen a lot of places and has spoken to a lot of people. Rerouting should not be worrisome. If one keeps driving, the destination will get closer over time.

Here is a guideline that can help our language learners in their journey. While this guideline is addressed to language learners, language teachers should modify the content as they see fit for their prospective language learners and the learning environment.

Your Path, Your Journey

> *The thin dog is running in the road, this dog is the road.*
> *- Virginia Woolf*

In what is known as Zeno's paradox, "You will never reach point B from point A as you must always get half-way there, and half of the half, and half of that half, and so on." Another fascinating feature in living and learning as art is that as we move towards something, it seems as though that thing keeps moving with us. It is a paradox because we seem to differentiate ourselves from things around us. When we learn, we make the path we walk on, so the path is walking with us. In a way, the path may seem external to learning, but in fact it has become internalized. It is not *a* path; it is *my* path. Like my finger is my finger and not a finger. My finger is my finger because although it may look like any other finger, it actually has carried only my life experiences in it and nobody else's. But more importantly, now my finger affords certain functions that some other fingers may or may not be able to execute. The fingers of a cook, not any cook, that particular cook, or that particular guitar player, or that particular painter is part of who that person is and how the person does things. The same is true with the path we create as we learn a new language. It is our path; we created it through our unique experiences, and it grows with us.

If we accept the notion that our learning experience is unique then we should also try not to compare our progress with that of others. As human beings, we tend to blame ourselves for any shortcomings in language learning. Even if the blame rests on us, everyone's circumstance are different. Another person may have more pressing reasons, more time, more experience, more exposure, etc. to learn a new language. Because someone learned a new language in two years, I should not expect myself to do the same thing. It is impossible to know the circumstances of someone's life and also to know to what extent they really know the new language. That artist's way is to compare yourself with yourself.

In the same vein, we can never compare learning one language with learning another. Languages are dynamic systems interacting with our previous acquired languages. We can never know the complexity of such interaction in advance. We can never be sure how knowing about sewing may help someone learn cross-stitching, embroidery, crocheting, knitting, or quilting. The same is true for someone who has any of these latter skills and now wants to learn sewing.

Similarly, we should not tell ourselves that we are incapable of learning a new language. All human beings, except those with serious neurological deficiency, speak at least one language. If we have done it for one, our native language, we can do it for another. While it is true that some people are more visual, verbal, musical, mathematical, or social than others, there is nothing blocking anybody to gain skills in any fields. They may just need more practice. Every normal person with fingers can potentially learn to play the guitar. The same is true with learning a language.

Curve Roads Ahead

Water running down a hill only knows that it will get down the hill some time and somehow. Seldom it is a straight line; most of the time it is meandering and full of obstacles that have to be overcome. Like water, we should never be afraid of correcting the path to our language learning journey. This advice is particularly important when a language learner is taking a test in language classrooms. The mistakes we make in a language test, for the most part, only reflects how much grammar or how many words we could memorize. Even when it is designed to do so, a language test is seldom a direct indication of the ability to use the new language. When making mistakes, we should remember how we learned to ride a bike, by falling and getting up to ride again, each time learning, one step at the time, first, how to maintain our balance and then pedal, and then get to where we intended to go. Language works the same way.

Sometimes stops means new starts. While on the road to learning a new language, occasionally we may feel slow progress or even lack of progress altogether. Even if there are no other problems, which we will discuss in the upcoming chapters, learning a new language frequently does not follow a linear progression. The terrain of language acquisition is usually uneven and occasionally requires detours. It is not only us taking on a road; the road is also taking on us, and we need to pay attention to its directions. We may start taking classes for the idea that we need an intensive grammar review, but later find out that what we need is more speaking practice. We should pay attention to our path to learning a new language, and let it redirect us if necessary.

To Be a Piano Player

Language learning, similar to most artistic and manual work, is a motor skill. In contrast to rote memorization, motor learning depends on repetition of a small routines, with the aim of precision. A ballet dancer does not learn five new dance moves in every class. The idea is to learn a bit at a time but to practice so many times that each move becomes as close as possible to a perfect move. Similarly, small children do not learn 100 new words every day. They spend most of their times fine-tuning the use of few until they know and can use them well.

In the journey to learn a new language, it is important to be consistent. Art is the pursuit of total control over our muscles. While it is possible to study pre-algebra one semester and return in a couple of years to continue with more advanced algebra, the same cannot be said about learning a new language. In most cases, we will have to start as a near beginner again if we have not been using the language in the meantime.

Following on the previous argument about motor learning, our nervous system dedicates a special resource to repeated and consistent learning, called *procedural memory*[2]. This is the type of learning that deals with *knowing how* rather than *knowing about*. If we truly want to learn *how* to play the piano, we must take the time to practice on a consistent basis, whether it is once a day or once a week. Interruptions and irregular schedules greatly diminish our capability to master any learning that deals with the use of memory muscles, whether it is our fingers or the vocal cords. We can take breaks if we must, but it is the consistency that moves us forward toward learning the new language.

Exploring the Journey

Now it is the learners' turn to discover their journey to learning a new language. Learning a new language is a big undertaking, and every individual must take the time to reflect on it. The questionnaire presented here attempts to evaluate the ways a language learner generally sets goals and follows through. These questions are intended to help language learners map their journey in a more realistic way, so they are more conscious about approaching and proceeding with future milestones in learning a new language. Learners are encouraged to avoid short and yes or no responses. They can write down anything that comes to the mind. It is especially important to provide examples from one's life experiences.

Each question solicits responses into two sections A and B. Responses in Section A are intended to explore one's overall tendencies and predispositions, especially from past experiences. Language learners are encouraged to avoid responses directly related to any language learning endeavor. In Section B, language learners are asked to reflect and predict how they plan to learn a new language. If they are just starting to learn a new language, they can explore similar experiences as those in Section A. If they have already started with the journey of learning a new language, they can try to use both the general experiences as well as particular involvements with learning a new language. They should attempt to explore similarities or differences in approaches that are helpful in this new undertaking. Learners should suggest to themselves the type of adjustment they need to make. They are asked to reflect, guess, and predict. The sample Blank Table is provided to organize responses.

An Example

The Sample Response is an example for the ways a learner can respond to this questionnaire. The first question asks, "Do you usually keep track of your upcoming agendas and activities with a

Sample Blank Table

Q:	A: Your Overall General Tendencies in Setting and Following up on Goals	B: Your Reflection on How You Can Plan for Learning a New Language
1.		
2.		
...		

planner or similar tools? If you do, how do you use them and for what particular agenda? If not, what are the reasons?" Of course, responses will vary from that shown here.

Sample Response Table

Q:	A: Your Overall General Tendencies in Setting and Following up on Goals	B: Your Reflection on How You Can Plan for Learning a New Language
1.	Yes, for small chores such as doctor appointments or work meetings, I usually use the Calendar app in my phone which also coordinates with my office computer. Depending on the agenda, I usually set an alarm for at least a couple of days before something is due. Also, for bigger projects that involves multiple deadlines and steps, I usually create a spreadsheet in my computer that would allow me to see the bigger picture and prompt me with the necessary actions I will have to take.	I think I can organize my language learning activities and objectives in the following ways. 1) I can create a planner to show the days and the amount of time that I will dedicate to study the new language. In the same calendar, I will also show the type of activity, e.g., active studying, doing homework, practicing with others. 2) I can also create a spreadsheet to show the progress and the content of the learning. For instance, I can schedule to focus the first 2 months on basic grammar and some conversation with an interactive app on my phone and then the next 3 months reinforcing the previous materials and taking an online language class.
2.	...	...

Questionnaire

1. Do you usually keep track of your upcoming agendas and activities with a planner or similar tools? If you do, how do you use them and for what particular agenda? If not, what are the reasons?
2. How often do you self-correct an agenda when it is not working the way you expected it? How do you do it?
3. Is it more important to you to follow through on the timeline you have set for yourself, or just to get the job done in whatever way possible? Why?
4. What tasks and goals are you willing to show some flexibility with and what are the tasks and goals that you will never compromise?
5. How often do you set your mind to do something and never follow through? What happens in such events?
6. Do you usually separate your goals based on short-term and long-term agendas? Are your short-term and long-term goals usually related?
7. Do you prefer to be very specific with your goals or leave room for possible changes?
8. Do you prefer to measure your success in concrete terms, or are you just happy with any sense of accomplishment?
9. If a task is big, do you ask for help or you rely on your own skills?
10. Do you usually reflect back on your previous tasks to see how you performed? If you do, what type of conclusions do you usually reach? If you do not, why do you think it is not necessary to reflect on previous tasks?
11. Has there been any aspect in a big project that seemed difficult for others but easy for you? What was it and why was that easy for you?
12. How would your friends, family members, and classmates/coworkers rate you for your consistency and flexibility for doing any project?

CHAPTER 6
Why: Motivation

A Light Turns On

As a very young kid, I was always curious about electricity. I could not fathom the idea that pressing a switch on the wall could turn on a light on the ceiling. I always wondered: how does this magic happen? Where does the light come from? How is the light connected to that thing on the wall? Why do we plug things into electrical outlets? How does the outlet make things work? I played a lot with electricity. My parents always scolded me and warned me of the dangers of playing around with electricity. Their warnings fell on deaf ears. Among many misadventures with electricity, I think at least a couple of times I touched hot wires with bare hands, with very unpleasant results. I had to experiment with things I was curious about.

In third grade, we were assigned to do a science project at home. The idea was to build a very simple electric circuit that would light up a small battery-powered bulb. The modest circuit consisted of a 3-volt battery, a tiny bulb, an electric switch, and some wires. With the help of my father, we bought the supplies from an electric shop. We also found a piece of wood to mount the pieces. We followed the directions in our science book to wire up the circuit. My father double-checked everything, and finally the moment of truth arrived. He allowed me to turn on the switch. It lit up! I was ecstatic. That day was probably one of the most memorable events in my life. I felt like I finally had the minimum understanding of how magic works. After that day, I became obsessed with electrical and electronic projects. By the time I was in the fifth grade, I would print electronic circuit boards, create my own custom-made mini radio station, and run many electronic devices on solar energy, and that was in the 70s.

While initially I studied electronics, my life took me to other fields such as psychology, cognitive and neuroscience, applied linguistics, linguistic anthropology, and semiotics. To this day, however, whenever I am tired of everything else, of all that academic reading and writing, and want to relax, I go to my closet full of electronic hardware and do something new with them. Maybe initially I was just a curious kid, especially about electronics, but what really motivated me to keep going was that I actually did something about it, acting and not just thinking, and it was always through tinkering and experimenting. At one point in our lives, we are told to stop experimenting and only to think about things. From then on, not only do we stop learning but we also lose our desire to learn. Learning becomes abstract; it does not solve anything; learning becomes just an appendage to our big brain.

IQ is Overrated

On the first day of all my language classes, I usually ask my students about their motivation to learn a new language. I ask them questions such as, "Say three reasons why you want to learn this language." Or, I instruct them to write, "How will learning the new language improve your life?" The content of their responses and the way they articulate them give me a lot of feedback about their initial disposition and the likelihood that they will succeed in acquiring the language. But more importantly, I think these questions allow the students to find out for themselves about their motivation. Learning a new language is a very big undertaking without many rewards along the way, especially at first. If the goal is to become fluent in the new language, there will be weeks, month, even years of frustration ahead. A lot of language learners blame themselves; they assume that they are not smart enough, and they give up on learning the new language.

Unfortunately, most language learners think that there is a direct relationship between general intelligence and learning a new language. There may be some connection between general intelligence and learning, not only with learning a new language but for everything. However, general intelligence does not, in anyways, guarantee a fast route to language acquisition. There are many reasons for the lack of such correlation. However, it is sufficient to mention that even at the purely cognitive level, language acquisition is a type of learning that does not rely heavily on introspection or general intelligence; rather, as it was discussed in previous chapters, it is more of a motor skill that requires repetitive practice, like playing the piano. I think anyone can look around to find many instances of highly intelligent people who breezed through all other subjects at school but came to a standstill when they had to learn a new language.

There is no other factor more important in learning a new language than the reason for pursuing it. Although it is frequently mistaken for other types of learning, learning a new language is not like learning math or computer programming. It falls into a totally different category of learning that is unique in many respects. The reasons why someone wants to learn a language can make all the difference in the world. It can also be the best predictor of gaining fluency in a new language. Therefore, it is not surprising to find that much of the research in a second language acquisition is related to motivation[1]. In this chapter, first I will lay out some of the aspects of motivation from an artistic point of view and then provide a guideline so you can also help your own language learners.

In the Driver's Seat

The gap between a novice language learner and a competent speaker is wide and deep. This difference is especially evident for adult language learners. While it is always cute to hear an 18-month old baby babble and speak in broken phrases, such as "me hungry," or "daddy bye-bye," nobody expects to hear an adult communicating at that level. It is not even about the broken language; an adult's language reflects an adult's thinking. They are expected to use language to hold a 10-minute conversation with many people at a party, negotiate a good price at a car dealer, and write a report at the end of the workday. A baby will never achieve this level of communicative competence.

Most adults are used to seeing the fruit of their labor within a short time in many fields. They soon grow impatient and frustrated when they notice that language learning does not give them an immediate result. When students take a year of algebra, a rather complex learning task, they can move on with other more difficult mathematical concepts. In contrast to language, most learning skills have milestones that provide a sense of progress. After a short training, anyone can learn the basics of plumbing and over time add to their skills. In the first year of working as a plumber, a plumber is still a plumber. But in the first year of learning a new language, the learner is not a speaker of that language. If they are studying in a classroom, it will take considerable effort and persistence to reach a proficient level in speaking the new language.

Types of Motivation

Looking into the reasons for why people want to learn a new language has been exhaustively investigated for at least the past 60 years[2], and it is the most single important topic in second language research. Study after study has shown that most people will, at some point, give up learning a new language unless they are highly motivated. Current research divides motivation into two types, *Intrinsic* versus *Extrinsic* motivation[3]. Others have alternatively called them *Integrative* versus *Instrumental* motivation[4]. They are similar concepts. The idea is that in intrinsic or integrative motivation, people have a positive attitude towards the new language and its culture. They want to learn a new language because they like it. In contrast, in extrinsic or instrumental motivation, people view learning the new language as an opportunity to gain something else. Language is just an instrument to get them a better grade, job, status, higher education, or income. In other words, learners are motivated to learn the new language not because of the language but for other benefits that come through it.

The Art of Motivation

While creating categories for types of motivation in learning a second language is useful theoretically, it does not help the learner in any practical ways. Again, a scientific view of language acquisition starts from the perspective of the scientist looking into an objective world and not from individual language learners interacting with their subjective outlook toward the world. What does it mean for language learners if they have extrinsic motivation? If anything, it works against their motivation to learn the new language because it puts them in a certain framework with fixed parameters. In a way, the linguists are telling most language learners that they can never love the language because this is who they are: a language learner with extrinsic motivation. On the flip side, there is the assumption that those who love the language and its culture never intend to gain practical benefit from it; they just love the language. God forbid if they intend to use the new language to increase their income or to use it while traveling; they are just intrinsic learners! Of course, read that last part with a sarcastic tone.

Yes, initial motivation to learn a new language does matter and should be taken into consideration. However, both language learners and language they are learning interact and change through time. The initial motivation for starting a class in playing the piano, drawing still life, practicing martial arts, or flying an airplane might be very different during the early learning process than when the person gains mastery in those skills. The reason is that the piano, oil painting, martial arts, and flying an airplane also influences and changes the person. Everything we learn, every skill, every experience changes us. If we take the painting out of a painter, this is not the same person anymore. Painting has become part of that person and his or her personality. The same goes for learning a language. The new language at one point becomes a part of language learners, and whether they grow to love it or hate it might not necessarily correlate with how they felt about it in the beginning.

Desire, Yearning, or Motivation?

From an artistic perspective, the word *motivation* does not really convey what is meant as a driving force, at least not in a sense intended for learning a second language. The word *motivation* is very dry, scientific, and *boxed-in*. In fact, the words *motivation, motion, movement,* and *motor* come from the same root. That alone should tell us the mechanistic meaning of the word *motivation*. Probably the word *desire* is preferable. Motivation has a definite beginning and ends. Desire is open-ended; it implies that we are drawn toward something unseen and constantly developing, that down the line we may be surprised to find something new. Motivation is for something; desire is for itself. Motivation may come with regrets and failures; a desire does not waste its time in self-pitying acts of regret. Motivation may never lead to anything more than what it was intended for. Desire can connect to many other roads. Motivation assumes that we already know why we are doing something. Desire recognizes that our very small act, what we are doing right now, is only a small step toward a much bigger longing. We rationalize our motivations, but desire is driven by our intuition and subconscious mind that sees our whole existence toward a much bigger goal, maybe self-actualization. But more importantly, motivation is discouraged by troubles, obstacles, and negative feelings. Difficulties, blocks, and drama, however, can be fuel for desire.

Why Do We do Anything?

If we think of the reasons for learning a language, just in terms of a very limited, finite, and narrow goal, then, of course, we might think about the reason in terms of motivation. But is this even possible? Is it possible that, for instance, our motivation for going to college is only about getting a degree, but not tapping into our intellectual capacities, having better job opportunities, receiving personal satisfaction, or making our parents proud of our achievement? And isn't it true that each one of those goals is also related to many other personal, familial, and professional goals? Isn't it true that, for instance, having better job opportunities and making more money is also related to the bigger goal of having a comfortable life? And isn't it true that having a professional degree and a nice job title is also related to our sense of prestige and self-esteem? Similarly, isn't it true that by receiving personal satisfaction and tapping into our potential capacities, we are also trying to be the best we can be, to have an inner feeling of fulfillment? Then how can we limit the reasons for learning a language to just a temporary and defined goal?

It is crucial to understand the interconnectedness of the goals and the chain of desires when pursuing any task in life. The problems associated with a lack of motivation in becoming proficient in a new language has a lot to do with this shortsightedness of not seeing the bigger picture of goals and desires. In a way, we have been missing this point when we tell our language learners that they are studying the new language in order to meet people from different parts of the world, or to facilitate business transactions when working in an international company, or to get admission for graduate work in a prestigious university, or to feel closer to the culture of the target language, or to give their brain a boost, or to read literature in the original language. These reasons are too definite and bounded.

The Science of Pleasure

Science approaches motivations from a neurological perspective. The assumption is that the nervous system assesses stimuli from the outside world as either rewarding or punishing and invites actions that bring us pleasure and rejects on activities that bring us pain or hardship. Hence, biologically speaking, we pursue rewarding events that are pleasant or novel, or that fulfill a physiological or social need. Conversely, we avoid punishing events that cause us pain or danger or tarnish our social image. It is believed that the autonomic nervous system (fight or flight) and the endocrine system (regulation of hormones) reinforce such mechanisms.

John Schumann, a professor of applied linguist at UCLA, and one of my Ph.D. advisers, has extended the mechanism responsible for general stimulus appraisal to the way learners are motivated to learn a second language[5]. Schumann believes that second language learners must find rewarding stimuli that encourage them to learn the new language. He suggests that a teacher, a teaching method, particular teaching contents, certain exercises, fellow classmates, the aspects of the target language culture, or the teaching devices use in the language learning process may play such a role.

I think Schumann has recognized that we are not merely a biological machine, responding to our external stimuli. Instead, he suggests that there is a link between human biology and our will to make something as pleasurable, such as specific features of learning a second language. I would like to take this argument even a step further. I firmly believe that all phenomena do not happen within things, in this case only in our nervous system, but between things. Hence the pleasure of learning a second language is neither in the learner nor in the features of the second language but between them. But let us first unpack this idea a bit more.

The Art of Desire

Science tends to confuse the medium with the action, the message, or the effect created by the medium. Although we need a hammer to hammer something, the hammer itself is not the act of hammering. It is true that for watercolor painting we must have some sort of paintbrushes, papers, and paints, but it is an understatement to say that painting made by a painter can be reduced to the elements needed for painting. The same analogy can be applied to the idea that it is the elements of our nervous system that motivate us to seek or avoid something.

In the case of motivation, it appears that in all living things, there is an underlying system that reinforces the action itself, namely, seeking pleasure and avoiding pain. However, there is no way to determine that it is the elements of the nervous system that promotes seeking pleasure and avoiding pain. It may very well be the case that the elements of our nervous system are consequences of other motivations, for instance, the desire for survival. But then we can ask: why do we desire to survive? What are, or rather where are, the neurobiological components of survival? Is the desire to survive in us, outside of us, or between us and the environment?

Let me give another example to illustrate this dilemma. We know that by taking certain types of drugs, collectively called *Selective Serotonin Reuptake Inhibitors*, or *SSRIs*, such as *Prozac*, we can relieve depression[6]. Prozac limits the amount of reabsorption of serotonin, known as the *happiness neurotransmitter*, between neurons. The abundance of serotonin in our brains can make us happier. However, we can safely assume that the depression was not initially created by lack of serotonin; rather, it was how a person reacted to an event in the outside world that was followed up by a certain chemical reaction in the nervous system, one that now the individual has to offset by taking Prozac. While we all share more or less the same nervous system, people vary widely in terms of how they perceive something as depressing or joyful. Hence, we cannot say that it is the nervous system that makes a person depressed. The nervous system is only the media through which phenomena are brought into existence, namely psychological states.

But it is also true that pleasure and pain are not in the external objects in the world either. Even a torturing device can only inflict pain when it is used for that purpose. It has no pain in it, per se. Similarly, the pleasure of enjoying a painting cannot be in the painting itself, since most animals with a perfect functioning nervous system would not care for a painting by Monet or Picasso; it is only certain people, and not all, that by looking at such objects would experience pleasurable states. In the same way, language contents, teaching methods, certain instruments, or assessment styles, as objects or media, cannot in themselves be pleasurable or painful for language learners. Every learner reacts to any of the above elements differently.

Now, if the experience of pleasure and pain is neither in the person nor in the objects, then where is it? This is to say, if the experience of joy in listening to Chopin is neither in the piano nor the sound waves from the piano nor in the ear of the listeners, then where is it? Similarly, we can ask if the motivation in learning a new language is neither in the learner nor in the materials and teaching methods then where is it? These are very valid questions with some very important philosophical implications. But let us avoid the philosophy for the time being and explore the importance of this question in the context of our language learners.

In the Middle

> *The thirsty person groans, "oh where are you the tasty water, and the water cries back, where is someone to drink me." It is because of the water's attraction that we have thirst. We are for it and it for us.*
> *- Rumi: Masnavi: Book 3, 4398*

One way to understand where something happens, whether it is the pleasure of listening to Chopin's music or learning a new language, is to look for those effects not inside but between things. Effects are always the results of exchanges and interactions, in the middle of things. Artistic abilities can help us understand this idea much better than other skills. For instance, the beauty of a song is neither in the song nor in the person who hears it, since one person may find one song more interesting and another person some other songs. A song may only trigger something in someone. We can extend the same idea with paintings, dance, and even romantic relationships, jobs, and, yes, with learning a new language.

The idea of interaction between the object of desire and the person who desires something has great implications for the understanding of our likes and dislikes. Many people berate cubism, or abstract arts in general, as nonsensical or rich people's art. The claim is that sometimes people appreciate something as art only because it is expensive, or when they are told that it is artistic.

In a frequently cited example, Marcel Duchamp, a French-American painter and sculptor, presented an object as a piece of art to the Society of Independent Artists, to be shown in the Grand Central Palace in New York City. The object was titled, *Fountain*[7]. What did not first come to the attention was that *Fountain* was a man's urinal rotated 90 degrees. When rotated that way, *Fountain*, a man's urinal, actually resembled a good-looking fountain. Some people still use the *Duchamp's Fountain* as an example of an anti-art cultural movement to claim that art is sold to people as art, and that frequently there is no inherent quality that makes an object "art." What these people miss is that they think that the effect of art and the object of art are the same thing. They are not. To be fascinated with something is an effect that happens *between* an observer and an external entity. It is neither in the person nor in the entity. Of course, not all objects can create fascination and not all people can be fascinated regardless of what they are being presented with. Certain objects tend to create more fascination in more people, but the fascination itself is in neither. Fascination, obsession, appreciation, attraction, enchantment, love, and motivation are transcendental and subjective effects. They are the emergent qualities that arise from and between two sentient beings or between a sentient being and an external object.

Motivation is the action part of the fascination, obsession, or being in love. It is when we finally get out to do something about our obsession and experiment with it, like I did with my early electronic experiments, explained at the beginning of this chapter. But interestingly, even fascination, obsession, or being in love is also in the middle of two other things. In a way, everything is always in the middle of something. And in this case, fascination or motivation is in the middle of the emotion of loving and doing something for loving. Our love for something or someone can only grow when we do something about it, and the more we do something about it, the greater love we *may* get. A word of caution is needed here, that the modal 'may' was intentionally put there; we may receive greater love. But without doing anything about our love, we are guaranteed to waste it. Anyone who has ever been in a serious relationship can testify to this fact, that love comes with hard work.

It Takes a Village

The hard work that we put into something we love does not feel like labor. It is not goal-oriented either. It is purely a joyful engagement, a kind of pleasure that lasts for a long time. It is not grit for the sake of being gritty. Once while driving I saw a billboard that read, "Parenting, the hardest thing you ever love doing." Any parent can relate to this slogan. Parenting is anything but easy. But we do not become parents because it is easy. Nor do we become parents because it will make us rich or give us certain benefits or present us with a lifetime achievement award at the end. If anything, it is the hardship of parenting that gives us pleasure. Playing a videogame, on the other hand, may give us a fleeting pleasure, but seldom does it leave us with a satisfactory and enduring feeling of joy and happiness that comes with raising a family or getting a university degree.

But more importantly, many hard things such as parenting are joyful because they change us, and we usually grow through them and with them. A child goes through different stages of development to finally become an adult, from a newborn to a toddler, to a preteen, to a teen, and finally to an adult. Through all these stages, the parent is not the same parent. He or she is also a different parent, a parent growing and developing to learn how to become a parent for all these different stages. In other words, it is not only the parent who is teaching things to a child; it is also the child who is teaching a parent to be and act like one. It is a dynamic and interactive process of learning and growing together. This is, for the most part, where the enduring joy and pleasure come from.

Similarly, language learners are in an interactive and dynamic process of growing with the language they are learning. We have to start thinking and seeing it that way. The new language is parenting us, raising us, and nourishing us. In turn, we are making the new language act as a parent, to feed us correctly at every stage of our learning, from infancy to adulthood. We should tell our language learners that they are not in it because it is easy, and they should not be looking for shortcuts and hacks to grow. There are no hacks to raise a child from an infant to an adult in 3 months, and language learners should not be looking for similar hacks in learning a new language. The hardship can turn into an enduring pleasure if they start enjoying the process rather than the results. In a symbolic way, the language looks back at a language learner and think to itself, "What a cute baby! Look how hard he/she is trying." But the language is only willing to parent us and call on all of its parenting skills as long as we commit ourselves in a long-term parent-child relationship.

The language is not alone in this parenting endeavor. It does take a village to raise a child. A language belongs to the community of its speakers and all of its resources. The Spanish language is not in one language teacher, one book, one app, one class, one neighbor who speaks the language, or one trip to South America. But it is at the same time, at least partially, in all of them. It is highly rewarding and motivating to experience the step-by-step progress and interaction with the community of a new language, from recognizing the alphabet and being able to read signs of a store or billboard, to order food in a restaurant, to enjoy a song in the new language, to write a text message on the phone, to read a short story in a magazine, and who knows maybe one day even to give a presentation or write a poem in the new language.

The new language will call on all its resources if the learner show commitment in a mutually nourishing relationship. Any language is an accumulation of its people, history, wars, peace, famines, success, stories, poems, dramas, and gossips. It will give all it has if the learner shows that he or she is not there just because there is a job offer with a string attached that requires knowing Chinese or Spanish. The new language is not a disposable wipe to clean dirty hands with and throw it out after use. If the new language is treated with the respect that it deserves, it will nourish the learner for life. The motivation to learn a new language rests on this respectful relationship. The learner is not just learning new words and grammar, but a world of experiences expressed through words and grammar. The learners will be highly motivated to learn a new language if they can only cultivate this appreciation in themselves.

Exploring Learners' Motivation

The following questionnaire is meant to help language learners discover their motivation to learn a new language. As a language educator, you can disseminate this questionnaire to your students. Understanding why we do things in life depends on who we are, what we aspire to do, what kind of previous experiences we have had, and when in life we embark on a new project. Furthermore, we all may start with a project for a particular reason but later develop a different incentive for it. There are no general standards or variables that can accurately assess everyone's motivation for doing something, including learning a new language. All we can do is to probe ourselves with prior experiences and initial tendencies, and from there, take it one step at a time. This questionnaire intends to reveal such aspects, so language learners can see for themselves where they stand and what they need to do if they intend to learn a new language.

The questionnaire is divided into two separate parts, Part A and B. Part A of the questionnaire intends to explore learners' motivation and aspiration for general projects and ventures in life, especially based on previous experiences. Part B of the questionnaire intends to specifically discover their intentions and ambitions for learning a new language. It is possible to browse through these questions first, but the best approach is to provide comprehensive responses at a more convenient time. Learners can think about their previous projects and ventures. Then they can start taking notes for each question. I suggest avoiding yes or no responses as much as possible. The responses to Part A may shed light on many aspects of Part B of this questionnaire. Based on the demography of your learners, you can pick and choose any questions from the list. However, make sure that you actually pair the same questions from both Part A and B.

Every person is different. This is not about making a negative or positive judgment about the learners' motivations, plans, or persistence. Rather, this should be looked at as an opportunity for learners to understand themselves and set realistic goals. In this chapter, I have laid out what it takes to learn a new language. Learners can review their responses with the requirements for learning a new language. They can evaluate their current situation and qualities to get an idea about the things they can rely on or improve on.

An Example

The questionnaire allows for open-ended responses. These responses can vary from one person to another. The first question in Part A of the questionnaire asks, "In general, how do you become interested in a new activity or project? Why?" My response to this question is: "I usually become interested in a new activity or project by its relation to an ongoing activity. For instance, if I am already involved in writing a new book, I may take on learning about podcasting, which I think can help me with reaching out to my readers. Occasionally, I become interested in very original projects. But in all cases, I always feel that any major undertaking that I pursue must both relates to a bigger project that I am involved in and also to give me certain personal satisfaction." Now, I can reflect further on this response about the peculiarity of my general motivation and how such characteristics can help me in future endeavors. Additionally, I can elaborate on features that I should change or improve to better accommodate a future project. For instance, in this case, I can state: "It seems that in general I am open to new projects as long as it satisfies my intellectual need and, in some capacity, relates to my bigger plan. Probably, I should avoid projects that are dull and may spark small and fleeting interest."

Questionnaire

Part A:
1. In general, how do you become interested in a new activity or project? Why?
2. For what types of projects do you get excited and soon lose interest? Why do you think this is the case?
3. How do you generally perform in a project that you are required to do but might not be able to enjoy?
4. Can you usually enjoy or experience pleasure from very small progress from a big project?
5. When you start a new activity or project, do you usually expect it to bring you practical utility, personal satisfaction, a mix of these, or something else?
6. When starting a new adventure or project, do you usually look for the end result, enjoy the process, or both?
7. Have your interests and satisfaction with a project changed or evolved from its initial state? Do you recall a specific project? Explain how it happened.
8. Everything else being equal, does the duration of a project (whether it is a short, medium, long term project) influence your decision to follow through or quit it?
9. Other than the time commitment, what else makes you

give up on a project you are halfway through? Why?

10. How comfortable are you to receive constant feedback, correction, and criticism? Do you find these elements discouraging to the point of quitting a project?

11. Are you usually driven by your expectation of yourself or by what others think about you?

12. How much influence do other people (friends, family, coworkers, classmates, etc.) usually have on you in pursuing or quitting a project?

13. Has it happened to you to quit a project because it was not your highest priority? What happened?

14. Do you think it is better to be persistent and follow through projects despite lack of interest or quit a project when you have lost interest? Do you recall an incident from memory?

15. How do you in general handle uncertainty and ambiguity in a project? If it was up to you, would you participate in such projects?

Part B:

1. What made you first become interested in learning the new language?

2. If you did not have to learn a language for practical reasons, would you still do it? Why?

3. Has your interest in pursuing a new language ever changed? In what ways?

4. What do you expect from learning a new language?

5. Is your goal just to get by in the new language or gain full competency? Why?

6. If at one point you are still interested in learning the new language, but it is not a high priority, would you abandon it or keep going? Why?

7. If at one point you lose interest in the new language, will you keep learning to achieve your initial goals or will quit?

8. How discouraging is it for you to find out that in comparison to other people you are doing very poorly in learning the new language? Do you usually compare your progress with others?

9. What are the chances of quitting a language program if you think you are doing poorly?

10. How discouraging is it for you to receive constant correction in the new language?

11. How likely are you to go beyond your comfort zone to learn a new language, for instance, speaking with people you have nothing in common with, reading books you are not interested in or being in situations where you do not know what to say?

12. How learning a new language can influence other aspects of your life? In what ways?

13. Other than practical and intellectual benefits, in what ways do you think learning the new language can change you as a person? Guess and explain if you need to.

14. How interested are you in the culture of the new language (literature, arts, customs, traditions, celebrations, etc.)?

15. Do you feel that you can adapt part of the culture of the new language into your lifestyle? Which ones?

CHAPTER 7

How: The Method

Searching for the Best Method

Watching movies is an excellent method to learn a new language. At least this is what I used to think. Before leaving for Chile, I bought some Chilean movies on DVD. I thought maybe I could try learning Spanish through watching films. The good thing about DVDs is that they come with a lot of extra features. One of such common features is to allow viewers to add subtitles in different languages. Also, in contrast to watching a movie in theaters, it is easy to pause, go back, and fast forward a movie in a DVD format. Like a good language learner, every night, I loaded a Chilean film into my computer DVD player and sat down to watch the film, switching between subtitles in English and Spanish. I would first play a very small segment of a conversation between actors, pause, and then compare the conversation in both English and Spanish.

Although I used this method for only a couple of months, I think I learned quite a bit of Spanish in a short time. But more importantly, I did not have to force myself to sit down and study; I was actually looking forward to my nightly routine of watching a film.

Later, when my students would ask me about a good method to learn a new language, I would frequently suggest watching movies with subtitles. To my surprise, I noticed that many did not find that method interesting or efficient. Some were not interested in foreign movies. Some thought that maybe at some point they would try this method, but at that moment, they did not have the necessary competency to watch a movie in its original language. Some told me that watching a movie might be fun, but first, they needed something more concrete, for instance, a class with instructions geared toward really good grammar. Finally, others told me that by watching a movie they could improve their listening skills but not so much their speaking skills. I think they were all right. However, as a specialist in the field of language acquisition, I was constantly confronted with language learners who wanted to know about the best method of learning a new language. I did not know what to tell them.

Everything Else Being Equal

We live in the world of life hacks. Everybody wants to know the fastest, the easiest, or the shortest way to do things. Social media and personal blogs are full of short articles that promise their readers to achieve anything by following 5 or 10 steps. I cannot tell you how many times I have been asked about the best method to learn a new language. Language learners believe that there is a secret in learning Spanish, French, Russian, or Persian. There is no such a thing as the best method of learning a new language that can be true for everyone. Even if there is a method that is good for everyone, probably that method is not best for any single person. There is no one-size-fits-all in language acquisition.

The problem of the best method of learning is not unique

to learning a new language. It spans across all types of learning. However, similar to all learnings, most language learners look beyond themselves to find a solution. They usually think that efficient learning depends on pursuing the best method of learning, getting the best teacher, or reading the best book. I don't blame them. In mainstream educational research, humans are perceived as cognitive machines or computers who only process information. From such a perspective, of course, methods of processing can influence how we retain information. With trial and error, researchers and academics have tried to fine-tune their methods to make learning a new language faster, easier, and more efficient for language learners. I do not intend to criticize the existing methods of teaching a new language. I think there is validity in most methods. However, often, the underlying assumption about learning itself is that learning is only the processing and storing of information. Seldom is the learner conceived as an individual who can actively influence the learning process and method.

An Exit Strategy

At the end of a class, I often ask students to fill out an *exit card*. Students write a very short paragraph about they learned during the session. The activity serves at least two purposes. First, it is a quick reinforcement strategy. Writing what they have learned during the class can function as a reinforcement for important aspects of the learning content. Second, as an instructor, I receive immediate feedback from my students about what stood out for them. In other words, I do not have to wait until a midterm or final exam to assess my students' knowledge about the content materials. By quickly reading through their cards, I get an idea of how to adjust the lessons for the next class.

Exit cards have been a lot more useful to me than I had anticipated. By running this activity for many years, it has come to my attention that within the same lesson and for the same teaching materials, the contents of exit cards differ widely. I thought that since I was teaching the same thing to everyone in the class, I should expect similar results on the exit cards. But this is not usually the case. For instance, I have noticed that students vary widely on what they think is the most important part of a lecture. Yet, more striking is the fact that even those students who write about similar learning events differ in regard to what and how they understood something. It is very evident that, for instance, students' prior knowledge, even if it is not directly related to the topic at hand, somehow interacts with what they presently learn. As an educator, it is very clear to me that learners are not just a cognitive machine; they bring themselves into what they learn. The exit cards have shown me that what I teach is not necessarily what students learn. In short, learners pick and choose what to learn and how to learn based on their previous life and learning experiences.

The Art of Assembling

Sometimes, as language learners and teachers, we wrongly assume that a language class is like a factory assembly line, where learners are *received* in a very similar initial state and teachers only have to add parts to them, in this case, more grammar and vocabulary. Then, they are *passed along* to the next teacher or book to get even more parts. The struggle to find the best method of learning a new language comes exactly from such a mindset. Car factories do not see any reason to differentiate between cars going through the assembly lines and therefore look for a method to process the cars more efficiently, usually to produce more cars in a shorter time at a lower cost. In fact, many language instructional materials are designed in the same way. There is little or no feedback between learning and teaching. Learners are assumed to only receive and not to give.

Language learners are not cars, and language learning is

far from being an assembly line. Metaphorically-speaking, the language-learning experience leaves a lot of bumps, scratches, and cracks on learners' bodies. They become anything but those shiny and geometrically shaped parts you would find in the assembly lines. People learn a language in their particular way. Languages also change and evolve through time to adapt to the needs of their learners. When learners are confronted with a new language, both the language learner and the language attempt to figure out things together (see chapter 3, language as a semi-living organism). It's not a one-way encounter. There is no one method of interacting. The learner and the language offer each other useful things and ask the other to come closer, both collectively and individually, as language learners and as an individual language learner, and as a language collectively spoken by a group of people and as one language, the way one language learner speaks it personally.

From Baguettes to Sliced Bread

Even if there was one best method of learning a new language, over time that method would start to degrade and become less efficient. Let me give you some examples. Think, for instance, the way the famous French baguette bread made by bakers in small towns in France has evolved into precut bland loaves of bread we buy in the supermarket these days. Or, imagine the way colorful handmade Persian rugs have turned into dull office carpets. You can see for yourself the way Chinese calligraphy has changed into simplified characters typed into the computer keyboards. In these examples, the quality of an artifact suffers significantly when something is produced not for a person and by a person but mass-produced for the masses.

There is an interaction between the person and the product that is usually lost in mass production. What happens between an artisan and a product is different than what happens between a machine and a product. Mass production by machines is most efficient. However, the average person can see the difference between an artisan's production and machine production. We can see the process and history. We can see what we lost and what we gained. The production becomes more efficient at the expense of details.

However, other than quality versus quality, something else happens between an artisan and a product that usually goes unnoticed. I am not sure if we are aware that when a baker makes bread, that individual baker leaves part of himself or herself in the bread. That bread is a bit different than any other bread some other artisan baker has made. And similarly, the product leaves a bit of itself in the artisan. Making individual loaves of bread changes the baker a tiny bit. By baking one loaf of bread at a time, that baker becomes a better baker. As if the bread were a living thing, it interacts and changes the baker.

In the same way, I am not sure if we are aware of the changes that have taken place from the art of acquiring a language to the industry of language education; what we have lost and what we have gained. I am not sure if we are aware that learning a language is, in fact, changing the language in the learner a tiny bit at a time, and that, in every step, it is still a complete language, a baguette made by a novice baker. Of course, we can see how the learner changes, a tiny bit at a time, when he or she speaks the new language.

When language is seen from a scientific and industrial perspective and not from an artistic perspective, language learners are never complete speakers because they are always missing some parts. The issue is not that they do not know; they may know. The problem is that they do not know how to use their knowledge in real situations. From an industrial perspective, the learners still do not know enough. So, they are encouraged to come back to get even more. The frustrating part is that even when they are assumed to be close to a complete speaker, they are more of a fake speaker rather than a real one. They are always the ladder of learning, and not the ladder of usage, starting from novice, to pre-intermediate, to intermediate, to high intermediate, to pre-advanced, up to the most advanced level. And nowhere along the path, they are considered or qualified to be a baguette. They are destined to be packaged bread, precut, prepared, and always pre-something.

The Non-Method Method

While theoretical approaches to language learning claim to have an overarching agenda, the methods, have been historically associated with four language skills. These are listening, speaking, reading, and writing[1]. Each method is very much related to one or two particular skill and hardly encompasses a language as a whole. But, of course, these are artificial categories and, more importantly, there are no boundaries between each skill. Reading is very much related to writing, and listening is related to speaking. Reading improves both listening and speaking, and the latter influences reading. And all of these skills are still dependent on another, less-frequently discussed skill, called pragmatics[2]. To give an example, vocabulary, grammar, and even pronunciation change when we have a casual conversation with a friend than when we are giving a business presentation. Context changes language in profound ways, a feature usually ignored in most scientific methods of learning a new language.

In contrast to a mechanistic and scientific method, an artistic mode of learning a new language encourages interaction between methods of learning and the language learner. I hope I have been able to lay a foundation for differences between a scientific approach to learning a new language as opposed to that of an artistic one in chapter two of this book. In short, a scientific method of learning a new language starts with two false assumptions. First, it assumes that humans are similar to containers that can be filled with learning contents, one step at a time. Second, it assumes that there is no interaction between the learner and the contents of learning. However, languages are dynamic systems created by us, and we, in turn, constantly toy with languages to make them perform different functions. Learning a new language is similarly a toying process. New language learners are continually poking the words, grammatical structures, and the sound system of the new language to see how they can achieve certain functions with their communicative partners. Interlocutors who speak the new language, in turn, give constant corrective feedback to the learners, so they understand what they can and cannot do. Hence the whole learning objective is a moving target. There is no one way to hit the bullseye. The learner must constantly adapt to both the content and the method of learning.

But, of course, I understand the frustration of new language learners. They need structure; they require organization; they want to know in advance about the next step and possibly the whole path to proficiency. But an artistic way of learning a new language does not translate to chaos and disorganization. It just requires surrendering to the idea that we are not computers and the language we are learning is not similar to math equations that we have to memorize. It means that as we start walking on this path of learning a new language, we are ready to fall and get up, take turns, pick up and leave stuff on our way, and let the path tells us where we should go next. I cannot tell you how to do this and neither can anyone else. As language teachers, all we can do is to put forth certain guidelines for new language learners to discover their methods and change the method through time.

Some Guidelines

The following is a general guideline for methods of learning a language from an artistic point of view. These recommendations are not meant to prescribe one method over another but to delineate a path for self-exploration.

To Be and To Do

Learning is being and doing, not so much thinking. Even abstract learning is based on prior experiences. Our thoughts, perceptions, and sensations are all grounded in the sensorimotor system, the part of the nervous system that detects information from our surroundings and acts on it. The famous French psychologist, Jean Piaget, documented that children gain most of their early knowledge about the world by grasping, tasting, smelling, listening, and seeing things. Piaget recognized that such knowledge is not the passive processing of information. It is not listening or touching per se that brings knowledge to us; it is the bodily interaction with such external stimuli[3]. Most of the things we know are not only in our brains; they are experiences distributed throughout our bodies. Similarly, a new language does not reside in the brain. Learning a new language is essentially a bodily experience that comes through all of our senses. When we learn a new word, when we actually do, we have lived it; we have experienced it. As language educators we should provide opportunities for our learners to live the language rather than store it in the brain.

To Be Viral

Evolutionarily and historically, viral infections are the most successful method of survival and transformation. While almost all kinds of bacteria life can be killed by using antibiotics, there are very few anti-viral solutions to get rid of limited number of viruses. One good reason why viruses are so successful is that they are not really a fully living thing.

Viruses only live when they are part of another organism. Viruses insert themselves inside a host, put their genetic materials into their cell, and use the cell to their advantage to reproduce their RNAs and proteins. This can teach us something very important about the method of learning a new language: we are not retaining things in raw but only processing and passing them around. Although they may seem to be the same words, language parts that we have learned from someone are not the same that go out of our mouths when we speak or write them. When we truly use the new language, we have already changed the words of that language, from symbolic signs that did not have initial meanings, to references that now stand for something; they point to real objects, ideas, and concepts. More importantly, now they do something, like those inert genetic materials of a virus that now turn into useful proteins. Language learning should follow the same viral method; learners should do things with language, to use it, to transform it, and to pass it around.

To Be Imperfect

Perfection may be the best skill for the execution of an order for a person in an army uniform, but it is the enemy of learning, all learning. Being imperfect is an important talent for language learning. Language learners are confronted with a host of problems to conjure up just one simple sentence. They have to find the right words (vocabulary skills), put them in the correct order (grammar), articulate them correctly (pronunciation), and make sure that the sentence they are uttering is appropriate for the context in which it is used (pragmatics), all in an ongoing conversation. It is humanly impossible to be 100% correct, 100% of the time. Nobody will come to speak a sentence in a new language with that kind of expectation. As it has been termed in language acquisition studies, *Tolerance for Ambiguity*[4] is the greatest knack for anyone who wants to learn a new language. We should allow learners to guess, ask, predict, modify, and experiment with language. It is the feedback they receive while they use language that allows them to improve, not the waiting until they know how to say it correctly.

To Be a Parrot

There is a general misconception that when we learn something, the information is stored somewhere in our brain, and all we have to do is to call out the information from the 'brain bank' back to our tongue to say it. This assumption is so wrong at so many levels. Most of this unfortunate assumption comes from the use of computer metaphors for human cognition. But this assumption is wrong even for computers. Such metaphors are used to dumb-down very complex issues into one-liner explanations. The neuroscience behind learning is very complex, and I do not intend to present another dumbed-down version of it. However, it is sufficient to say that information is not stored in any compartment in the brain. Rather, it is distributed along pathways between neurons, some with weaker and some with stronger connections between many points along the path. There is nowhere in the pathway that you can point out and say, "here is the definition of the word 'hermosa' in Spanish which means 'beautiful' in English." Nothing like that happens in the brain. And this is not only about words. In a very similar way, when we hear a sound, smell an odor, or see a face, in multiple instances and multiple contexts, our brain creates a network of associative references for those stimuli, for what they were and what response was needed. There will be a stronger connection along the pathway when there are more frequent instances between a stimulus and successful followed-up actions that are advantageous to us. The pathway keeps refining itself with each repetition. Every instance of repetition creates a more refined and automated response.

This is the artistic part of learning through repetition. Even when we think we have learned how to play a song with the guitar, by repetition, we still keep getting better at it, one small step at a time. The take-away lesson from all this is that language learners have to repeat the use of any instance of a language feature, whether it is a new word, a grammatical structure, or a sound of a word. They are not repeating the same thing; they are getting better. They stop learning when they think they have enough skills to get things done, a concept referred to as *Language Fossilization*[5] in language acquisition research. After that, they will learn nothing. So, they should be reminded to keep repeating with the intention of refining and adding to an already learned performance, whether it is the meaning of a new phrase, the function of a grammatical feature, or the pronunciation of a new word. Let them be a parrot.

To Be in the Middle

All actions happen in the middle of things, never within things. Similarly, all meanings are relational. When we pick a book to read, what we call learning happens between us and the book. Learning is neither in the book nor in us. The interaction creates meaning and learning. If we pick a book and read it without the intention of doing something to it, no learning will ever happen. It is the intentional interaction with something that creates learning. Language learners can spend their entire lives listening to foreign movies in the original language. They will never learn anything unless they make an effort to intentionally use the contents of what is being said as learning opportunities and do something with it. The teacher, the book, or the online language program are not delivery systems for ready consumption. They have to be a part of that ecosystem of learning, always in the middle, processing, using, passing it on, and receiving it back for reprocessing and reusing. When language learners are presented with a new word, they should be encouraged to think about its meaning. Then we should allow them to use the new word in a new context and provide them with opportunities to receive corrective feedback. All reactions can be feedback, and learners can gradually modify their output to facilitate a smoother and more effective communication.

Repetition can also be very useful with grammatical

structures, most aspects of pronunciation, and pragmatic features such as politeness, intentions, implied meanings. This corrective process cannot be scientifically explained or described by simple or fancy equations or infographics. There is an art to such skill. Interaction and self-correction are more of a dance that requires constant coordination with slight changes. The more learners put themselves in the middle of the use of language, the better they get to dance it with others. As language educators, we should always place the language between the learners and the world around them.

Exploring Methods

In this part, I have provided a questionnaire that language educators can distribute among their learners. The idea is to allow language learners to explore an adequate method of learning a new language for themselves. Some questions may overlap with the questions presented in other chapters. Separating the method of learning from the content of learning or the reasons for learning is impossible. Learners can skim through the questions first. However, I highly suggest providing them with some time for each question. They should see these questions as a soul-searching activity, preferably in a place they cannot be disturbed. Each question solicits their responses into three sections, A, B, and C. Section A invites them to explore their overall learning preference, especially from past experiences. Section B is meant to help them discover their preferred method of learning a new language. If they are just starting to learn a new language, they can try to guess and predict. However, they can use their existing experiences if they have been involved in learning a new language for some time. Section C attempts to offer them a comparison/contrast between Sections A and B.

There are three objectives for this questionnaire. First, by responding to these questions, language learners can reflect on their particular method of learning, not that of their friends, classmates, colleagues, or parents. The second objective is to allow them to reflect particularly in terms of learning a new language. Naturally, some questions and responses could be similar for both sections. This is the third objective of this questionnaire, intended to be accomplished when working on Section C. In this part, they can try to figure out if there are similarities or differences between the way they generally learn something and the way they try to learn a new language. To better organize their responses, they can use the following table.

Q:	A: Your General Learning Methods	B: Preferred Method of Learning a New Language	C: Reflection on Similarities or Differences Between A and B
1.			
2.			
...			

An Example

In the next page, you will find an example of the way your students can respond to this questionnaire. The first question asks, "When confronted with a new learning task, do you learn it better on your own or from someone else? Why?" Here are a couple of potential responses. Of course, their responses could vary from those provided here.

Q:	A: Your General Learning Methods	B: Application for a New Language	C: Reflection on Similarities or Differences
1.	In general, I prefer learning things by myself because I feel in control of my learning flow and pace. Or In general, I prefer learning things from a teacher because I need someone telling me the steps and helping me along the way. I also feel that a teacher creates discipline, which I need for learning.	In contrast to general learning, I feel that it is essential to have a teacher for learning a new language because I need to have a correct model, for instance for correct pronunciation Or Similar to my general learning habits, I also need a teacher for learning a new language because a language teacher offers me feedback, to see if I am doing the right thing.	It appears that although I generally prefer to be an independent learner, in the case of learning a new language, I should try a teacher or at least a tutor in the beginning. Or Hum! It seems that regardless of the type of learning, I can get more things done with a teacher than learning on my own.

Questionnaire

1. When confronted with a new learning task, do you think you learn it better on your own or from someone else?

2. Who is your all-time favorite teacher? Why? Did he or she teach in a particular way that you liked? What did he or she do?
3. Do you prefer to learn new things through trial and error or step by step?
4. After you learn something new, do you prefer to act on it right away, or first see someone else do it? Why?
5. In general, what kind of environment is more conducive for you to learn something new: a quiet place like a library/your own room, or a classroom with many other people?
6. If you have to reinforce a lesson by repetition, such as using flashcards, do you prefer to repeat a small lesson over a shorter period, or a big lesson spread across a longer period?
7. What was the easiest way you learned something? What helped make it easy?
8. What was the hardest way you learned something? What caused the hardship?
9. What is your preferred learning medium, through written words, illustrations, or talk?
10. What kind of mnemonic devices do you generally use for learning new things (e.g., flashcards, acronyms, visualization, etc.)?
11. How important is it for you to use technology in your learning (websites, apps, eBooks, audiobooks, interactive programs, etc.)?

CHAPTER 8
What: The Content

> *You said,*
> *"Come,*
> *the garden and springtime are laughing in joy.*
> *And there are candles, wine, and lovers like idols."*
> *But none of these matters to me if you are not there*
> *And none of these matters to me if you are there.*
> Rumi: Robaiat, 913

Where Is My Liking?

I love poetry. It is difficult, however, to find people who share my passion for this fine art. For most people, poetry is just an elaborate form of talking. "It does not move me," or "I don't get all that symbolism and stuff," people often say. For most, poems do not have the kind of effect that novels, songs, or movies have. Maybe they are right. Maybe there is something universal about the type of content that creates more effect than other types. But

I am fairly sure that, at least in part, the effect has also something to do with the person. Or maybe the effect does not have to be either in the content or the person. It is possible that our interests, tastes, emotions, curiosities, attractions, or tendencies for things are not even partially distributed somewhere. Maybe they are created through our own doings and they keep changing through time. In fact, my love for poetry has changed a lot. I do not like some of the poems that I liked 20 years ago, and those that I still like, I like them for very different reasons than I did before. So, again, *where* is the liking for something? Where is that place that we can point our finger and say, "There it is my liking."

The 'Gardenness' in Us

Every time I come up with what I think is great content for teaching language I know that I am up for a disappointment. It is rather impossible to find something that everyone likes and can benefit from. But should a language teacher look for something appealing and useful to everyone? Is this even possible? Can we make our students like something? Or do we make any content interesting by the way we teach it? Is this about our teaching style or is it about the content? Language learners must have very similar questions. I am sure they keep looking for something interesting, challenging, effective, helpful, and probably real. They want to get the most out of their times when learning a new language.

As a second language teacher, we may even have additional questions. Should we use actual content that native speakers use that is authentic and dense in vocabulary and grammar but might be very difficult for language learners to understand, or should we use watered-down content that is easier to understand but not authentic, because it has been specifically devised for second language learners? Also, can we make our students interested in boring but instructionally-important contents by adapting games, so they can be used for language-learning purposes?

language teachers have many questions like these. In all these, we are asking the same question: What is educational content that is interesting and useful for all learners at the same time?

Rumi deals with the dilemma of content in a very elegant way in the poem I quoted at the beginning of this chapter. The garden, springtime, wine, candles, and "lovers like idols" are all nice. But all these are nice when we can do something with them that brings joy in a very particular way. In a way, Rumi is saying that a garden is not nice because gardens are nice; gardens are nice because we can bring out *gardenness* from a garden by involving and aligning our senses, memories, and behaviors into the activity of a garden. If we think of a garden as a joyous thing, then all the experience of joy must be in the garden. But this cannot be true. If you are running for your life because someone is pursuing you with a gun, a garden may not be a very pleasant place. However, if you think of the joy of seeing a garden as a function, then the joy of seeing a garden is at the intersection of two activities, a garden doing a garden activity and you doing an enjoying-a-garden activity. A garden is doing as much joyous thing to you as you are to a garden.

Snap out of it or into It?

A lot of well-intentioned language teachers try to make their content more interesting and effective by, for instance, implementing games and fun activities in their instructional content. The idea is to make language learning a more pleasant experience. This strategy reminds me of a song in the original Mary Poppins movie. Being a good nanny, Mary Poppins wants to convince Jane and Michael, two children she takes care of, that there is always an element of fun in every job, even in those seemingly boring household chores. She tells the children that finding that element can be easily realized, almost as fast as snapping the fingers. She then continues with her argument that sometimes taking a bitter medicine, a metaphor for a hard task, may need a spoonful of sugar, which I think stands for an element of fun.

There are many ideas about life in this song worth talking about. However, the most important point that relates to our topic is that a new language (the medicine) can be assumed as difficult in itself (bitter) which may need games and other types of entertainment (a sweetener, like sugar) to allow learners to absorb it. In a way, it can be expected that learning a language is a difficult thing and needs some sort of an external element to make it pleasant. I think what most people easily dismiss is the first part that maybe it is not so much the sugar that makes the medicine go done but the snapping part, which I think is a metaphor for changing our perception about the task at hand.

Yes, the first or the second time we teach a content through games is usually fun for learners. Most learners love it. Sometimes they barely even notice that they just learned something new. The problem is that games lose their utility and entertaining quality very fast. There is a rapid falling curve with using games as sugar to make the medicine go down; soon learners become numb to sugar and games. Games can't keep up with being entertaining all the time. So, we start to increase the sugar to keep the medicine still a pleasant thing to take. In other words, games, songs, crafts, and dance used as tools to learn a new language will lose their effectiveness over time. The reason is that using games as a medium of learning usually comes with the assumption that 'fun' or 'excitement' must be added in the content we use for learning. As the content loses its fun-factor over time, we keep looking for funnier or the funniest things. At one point we get to the place where we feel that we are not really teaching the language but just chasing fun. So, we start the cycle of getting rid of all the fun and looking for the most effective and instructionally-proven useful content. It will be dry stuff, but at least both the teacher and the language learners are happy to use their times efficiently. We just swallow the bitter medicine without any sugar. But then again, the learners get bored with dry content and become unmotivated to continue. So, again we start with adding more fun stuff to the curriculum. And this vicious cycle continues.

Avocados for a New Language

While I was in Chile, I personally experienced the known legend that Chinese food tastes different in every country. It is true. Chinese food tastes very different in Santiago, Chile than the meals I had tried in Los Angeles, California, in Vancouver, British Columbia, in Kaunas, Lithuania, and in Shanghai, China. I have a hypothesis for these changes in taste in different places of world. I think that Chinese restaurant owners have to make a difficult choice in the way they serve their local communities. One way they can approach their business model is to make very authentic Chinese food at the expense of losing many customers who might find very authentic Chinese food different than their own palate for food and hence lose interest. The second option is to compromise Chinese food with a mix of local flavors to attract more willing customers. After all, everyone is in business because of customers. If you do not have customers, you do not have a business. So, the Chinese restaurant owners, or all ethnic restaurant owners anywhere in the world, must find a balance between giving their customers something that can be accepted as Chinese or ethnic food while that food is still appealing to the local taste.

The way ethnic restaurants adapt their cuisine to the locals' taste is a good example to understand the complex relationship between authenticity and usefulness of contents in learning a new language. If I were a Chinese restaurant owner, probably at one point I had to ask myself to what extent would I be willing to give up the way Chinese food must be made at the expense of pleasing my customers. Where and how would I draw that line? The same uncertainty happens in the context of teaching a new language. As language teachers, it seems that we will have to draw a line between using content that is real language as it is intended for and used by native speakers, on the one hand, and a content that is made for learners of that language so that they are able to understand it, on the other.

Let me give you another example in the context of language education. Imagine a language learner who wants to learn Chinese by reading books. That learner can start reading Chinese novels intended to entertain adult native speakers of Chinese. This is real language, authentic and filled with cultural nuances that are highly important to know about Chinese life and culture. But this is not a very efficient way to learn Chinese, since those learners will have a hard time understanding anything from that content. They will have to constantly stop to look for the meaning of every word, idiom, and cultural reference. The learners will be bored to death after reading a page or so. They will be discouraged and probably give up altogether.

Or, the same person can start with books written for Chinese language learners, which of course are not real. Those books are only meant to teach the Chinese language. The vocabulary, the grammar, and the cultural elements are heavily watered down to please the learners. It may give them impression that they are learning Chinese, but those books teach a version of Chinese that no Chinese speaker ever speaks. In the real world, there is no such thing as beginner, or intermediate, or advanced Chinese. It is not even a Chinese restaurant in Santiago, Chile. It is more of a manual of how to make Chinese food. The question then is: what is Chinese enough for learning Chinese? What is French enough to learn French?

Instead of looking for authenticity, efficiency, the fun factor, or usefulness, I propose a different approach to content for learning a new language. All the above criteria assume that such features must be present in the content. Again, the learner is usually perceived as a passive recipient, who goes to the content and only takes something from it. We do not generally assume that the learner actually may bring something to the content. We forget that we bring *gardenness* to a garden. We assume that sushi is what sushi is. Californians have changed sushi, creating the California roll, as have Chileans with the excessive use of avocado in sushi rolls. In fact, I have heard that while not very popular, California roll is now offered in many sushi restaurants in Japan. The very things we call authentic, fun, tasty, useful, or efficient are constantly changing because we, the users, the consumers, the learners bring ourselves into the very thing we use and consume. We are active participants in what something is, whether it is food or language.

Some Guidelines for Good Contents

We change a song by singing it, a poem by reading it, a painting by looking at it, and, yes, a perfume by inhaling it. Although the artifact has not changed, there is a unique experience felt between us and the things of the world which is different from that of someone else's experience. Hence, every encounter is unique and as such creates a different effect, different 'fun,' 'usefulness,' and 'effectiveness.' A good painting is a good painting not because there is something inherently beautiful in it; it is good because it can create a lot of different effects in so many different people. That is, good art allows for a wider range of interaction and subjective experiences. The same can be established for content intended for learning a new language.

The following are some general guidelines when considering content for teaching a second language from an artistic point of view. The idea is that instead of prescribing effective content, that is effective in itself, we should look for content that can bring out effectiveness from the learners.

1. Interfacing Contents

Learning has mistakenly been associated only with books. We

assume everything we learn must come from words printed on papers, which are scanned by our eyes, and then magically stored in the memory cells of our brains. Of course, books are very good tools for learning, but they have many limitations that we should be aware of, especially in terms of learning a second language. First, a book-only approach to learning a language will not take the language learner very far. Learning through books is a passive approach that requires language learners to consciously reflect on the forms of language parts, meaning, and structure. Books do not allow for feedback. Book-learning is usually a one-way street, from books to learners. There is no one there in the book to correct learners' mistakes, emphasize their strengths, and nudge them along the way when they need it. Second, books are only good for receptive skills, such as comprehension. The new language can only become part of the language learners' behavior when they use, speak, and act on it. They cannot talk to a book, and unless they talk, they are not using language.

Ideally, contents for language learning must simulate a natural environment that allows for different types of media with different interfacing connections to our senses. In a natural environment, a child is exposed to multisensory information when learning a new word. For instance, in learning the word 'dog,' the parent frequently utters the word 'dog' while pointing to an actual dog or a picture of a dog. This learning event is then usually accompanied by mutual gaze at the dog. Parents also usually add other effects to this interaction, such as voicing a 'woof, woof,' sound, and a bodily imitation, such as walking on four. Parents are very theatrical with their children during the early stages of language acquisition. A lot is going on between a child and a parent that goes unnoticed. The pointing, the mutual gaze, the body position in space that allows for joint attention and interaction are essential elements in the product we call language acquisition. Most of these elements are usually lost or significantly reduced in books that only contain written text.

Whether it is a child acquiring a new word from a parent,

or a novice carpenter learning a new skill from a master, there is a whole ecology of interaction and interfacing between material objects and bodies that act together to produce a learning event[1]. Such rich interfaces are usually replaced with random use of media such as videos, sounds, images, and text in language classes. The assumption is that the use of more varied media and technology will produce better language learning outcomes. Technology and media are viewed as added features to learning, to enrich and entertain. However, instead of overwhelming the learner with more *things*, we should pay attention to the way objects interface with our cognition during learning events. For instance, the purpose of a spoon is to facilitate scooping and lifting the right portion of food and delivering it to the human mouth. A bigger, fancier, or multi-purpose spoon may or may not necessarily be helpful in this process. The usefulness of a spoon is not even in the spoon; it is between the spoon and the food, and between the spoon and our mouth. This is what it is meant by interfacing. Our desire for eating forces us to make an object, a tool called a spoon. At one point, when we learn to use a spoon to scoop food, that tool becomes almost an extension of our body. In choosing content for language learning we must also pay attention to in-between places, where our mind meets an object and makes the object an extension of its own, the human mind.

2. Drenching Contents

People have two approaches to the way they immerse their bodies in water. Some keep dipping parts of their body one at a time, while others just dive in with their whole body. While in both cases, the entire body will eventually get wet, these are two very different ways of experiencing water on the body. In the same way, walking in the light rain for 20 minutes is not equal to walking for 1 minute in torrential rain. While in both cases, it is the same water and the same body, the sum of the experience of each part of the body touching water is not the same experience of the whole body touching the water at once. Most experiences in life are not just added linearly.

Non-linear experiences also happen in learning. Learning is, after all, an experience. Reading a book in the new language for an hour a day over two or three days is not to the same as reading the same book for 10 minutes a day for 20 days. There is a drenching factor in doing something whole-bodily and whole-heartedly that cannot be experienced by adding smaller dipping or dripping experiences. The same goes for different modes of learning. There are fundamental differences in quality and quantity in learning a second language between two types of people who happen to live in the country where the target language is spoken. The first one sits on a couch in his or her hotel room and studies a language guide for two hours. In the same two hours, the second person goes to the street to take a taxi, orders a drink in a bar, and chats with the locals, all in the new language. While the person reading a book might get more language input, the person in the street is drenched in language, and it is the real use of language.

3. Becoming-a-Node Contents

In physiological terms, the human brain has not changed for at least the past 200,000 years[2]. However, there is no comparison between what humans have achieved with the same brain in the past 500 years as opposed to the previous 199,500 years. There is a reason for this. The intelligence to create all the science and technology that we have around us is not inside individual brains but between them. And what started this connection between the brains, for the most part, was the printing press, which by the way was invented around 500 years ago. When we read a book, we are not simply reading contents written by one person and one brain; we are basking in the glory of many minds connected, some with less and some with a greater degree of separation. In other words, since the invention of the mass media, one's intelligence depends on the number of connections he or she can make with other minds. It is the content that facilitates such connection.

Contents, like books, sound recordings, collaborative videos, and online apps, intended for learning a new language, are not created equal. There is a huge difference between the type of content at the levels of interactivity and type of interactivity. There is always a better chance to learn something new when there is more possibility of interaction between the material and the learner. However, learning a new language should progress both in depth and in breadth. It is not enough that a book teaches us a lot of new words; it should also aim to solidify the learning by allowing us to interact with the new words in different contexts and with more frequency.

The depth and breadth of interactivity for contents intended for learning a new language should also be applied to the type of connection. More connections usually come at the expense of looser connections and vice versa. Having a lot of friends usually means not having deep friendships, at least not with all of them. Similarly, with teaching, the idea is not just to expose learners to as much content as possible. A better strategy is to start with the content they are interested in and then let the content expand naturally to different directions using different media.

Let's say you are teaching French to English speakers. You show your students a French movie which was based on a French novel. They saw the movie with subtitles in English and loved it. Now, you can try to show them the movie in the original language. It will be difficult for them, but if they loved the dialogue and are determined, they will give a shot. The movie can also make them more interested in other books written by the same novelist. They may be interested to follow up on the songs in the movie, the lyrics, the singer, and more of the songs by the singer. If they liked the movie, there is a greater chance that they would continue with other movies directed by the same director, the songs from those movies, and more novels. One movie now can very naturally snowball into a greater depth and breadth with the French language, literature, and culture.

4. Losing-Your-Balance Contents

It is very unnerving when one starts to swim for the first time. Riding and driving for the first time are equally difficult. Walking for the first time must have been similarly challenging, but none of us remember that experience. We all learn quickly in all those activities for at least two reasons. First, in these types of learning, there are not that many transitional steps between not-knowing and knowing. If you are learning to swim, you either know how to keep your head above the water or you don't. Second, the stakes are high; you must succeed. While learning to swim, you do not want to have a high failure rate; your life is at stake. Learning a lot in a short amount of time has a lot to do with creating contexts that force us to lose our balance. One warning though: the higher stakes should more frequently favor success than failure. Otherwise, nobody would attempt to swim, ride, drive, or learn a second language.

In terms of learning a second language, we must also think about content that makes us lose our balance. Content that is challenging, unusual, puzzling, and original, forces us to constantly keep our head above water. We learn a lot from such encounters. In contrast, we won't learn much if learning is very safe, and making mistakes does not have real consequences. Learning one word at a time by reading books while holding a cup of coffee in the comfort of our living room is very safe, but we don't learn much, and whatever we learn, we will soon forget. If you change that type of learning with a live video conferencing with an international business partner where you must pay attention to every word and produce real-time concrete sentences in the new language, you learn a lot, very fast. The idea is that in learning a new language, the learner must be at least occasionally confronted with higher stakes and bigger risks.

Examples

Here are some examples of contents that have the potential to generate more interaction. While reading you can take notes to remind yourself of some more examples you could consider for your own learners. Write down the title of books and movies that as a class you can agree to read and watch. Think about the websites and blogs you can all visit. Reflect on potential audiobooks or podcasts. Remind your learners of human capital, such as friends, friends of friends, family members, colleagues, and classmates that can help them along with their language-learning journey. Start with a list. Later, you can add more items that work and delete those that won't.

1. **Non-content Contents**

Think outside of the box about what can be used as teaching/learning content. Although a bit dry, manuals for appliances can be some of the best reading content students can use to learn a language. Manuals usually include lots of drawings. Manuals allow students to understand the connection between the drawings and the language. Manuals also incorporate a lot of technical words that are very useful and usually missing in language instructional books. Other non-instructional but very useful contents are restaurant menus, travel brochures, and business flyers.

2. **Hyperlinkibility**

Web sites and blogs contain losts of hyperlinks that allow for greater interactivity. Orient your learners to get information from websites in the target language. Let them click on links to see where they land. The least they can do is try to find out about the nature of the site. Let them follow up on sites if they are interested in the information. Websites and blogs are a lot easier to read and understand as they are to the point, contain shorter contents, and implement diverse forms of relevant media, such as images, audio, and video.

3. Action

When teaching a new concept, let your learners act it out. Don't let them keep it in the brain. It won't be there for long if their body is not involved in the learning process. If it is a sentence, allow them to say it to someone. Let them get a response from another person and ask them to reply back. Create situations where they are the actors in a theater while simulating the conversation. Let them teach the new content to another learner or the class, for instance, in a micro teaching session.

4. Real

Use or create content from real life situations. Let's say, your faucet is broken, and you want to fix it. You will probably watch a YouTube video or similar sources. Use such occasions as a teaching opportunity. Let learners watch the video in the target language. Videos have many advantages. You can pause, go back and forth, show them the objects, and even sometimes use the closed caption to reinforce words and the correct spelling.

5. Reactional

Find contents that make your learners react. Comic strips are one of the best examples. You cannot just read a comic strip as you read an ad; you must understand it and have some sort of an emotional reaction to it, such as finding it ridiculous, surprising, strange, funny, unexpected, disappointing, etc. Comic strips are also one of the best ways to understand cultural references in the target language.

6. Social Media

Technology has forced us to be short, to the point, and relevant. You be the judge if this is a good or bad thing, but social media is perfect for teaching a new language. Let them read content written for social media and then have them find partners they can communicate using social media, e.g., Twitter, Instagram, Facebook. Seldom will you find grammar police in social media, so they can concentrate on communication. More importantly, social media is highly interactive and requires fast reaction, which is ideal for language learning.

7. Puzzling

There is a good reason why so many people enjoy mystery and crime novels. In this genre, the reader is highly engaged in resolving and entangling a puzzle. I think this is at least one of the reasons why IKEA sells so much; by assembling furniture, the consumers feel that they solved a puzzle. It is like Lego for adults. You get some sort of satisfaction and pride that you were able to put a dinner table together. Similarly, look for contents that allow your learners to actively explore issues, uncover traps, and resolve problems. Mystery and crime novels are great, but so are spy movies, interactive journals, and some of the TED talks.

8. Emotional

Puzzles are wonderful because they tap into one of the humans' greatest emotions: curiosity. But we have a lot more emotions. Any content that provokes an emotional response is potentially a very good source of learning a new language. The same goes for any content that arouses our senses such as taste, vision, hearing, and smell. Songs, plays, poems, and love stories are some of the examples of these types of contents.

9. Creating Content

There is a famous saying that in the game of life one should not be a spectator but a player. It is also said that you truly learn something when you teach it. In both of these cases, we have taken a giant step from being a consumer to a creator, from a passive receiver to an active producer. No learning beats that. Dare your learners to create new content in the new language. Let them write a poem, a short story, or a business proposal in the new language. Sure, tons of fallings and mishaps are involved but so are a lot of meaningful learning opportunities.

CHAPTER 9

Who: Learners

*It was because of nightingale's delight that the flower finally fell in love
And now the flower is eager to be even more flirtatious
The nightingale learned singing from seeing the grace of the flower
Otherwise, there was no sonnet or song in its beak
Hafiz (Divan: Sonnet 277)*

A Solo Duet Flamenco

As educators, we usually assume that our job is to be in complete mastery of the subject materials. When we teach something, we must constantly do a role play between a teacher and a learner, trying to figure out how would I understand this thing I am teaching if I pretend that I did not know it. Role playing is not knowledge; it an art, but good teachers, like good actors, perform it intuitively. In this chapter I intend to take the learner's perspective and provide guidance for best classroom practices that involves the learner as an active participant in the creation of knowledge.

    In the movie, *El Amor Brujo* ("Love, the Magician"), the protagonist, Candela, is obliged by her father to marry José. But like all good romantic movies, she is madly in love with another man, Carmelo, a childhood neighbor. José dies in an accident and Candela can now marry Carmelo. However, Candela feels she would be betraying José in marrying Carmelo. She is troubled by the ghost of José who appears every night to dance with her. It seems that this is the only way Candela can free herself from the guilt of abandoning her husband. The movie shows the dance between José and Candela from two perspectives, one from the perspective of Candela, in which she is involved in a duet dance with the ghost of José, and another from the perspective of Carmelo, who is hiding nearby and sees Candela dancing, of course, all by herself.

    The choreography of a duet dance, like a duet flamenco, must be very well-rehearsed down to every little detail. Body movements between two dancers must be so well coordinated that at all times they should appear as though there are not two persons dancing but just one. However, even in very well-prepared dances, two dancers must constantly coordinate with their partners. If there is even a fraction of a second of hesitation or elongation of a move in one partner, the other partner cannot go on with the dance as rehearsed; he or she must also pause or elongate a dance move to make sure that both bodies are coordinated in time and three-dimensional space. In fact, if you pay close attention to both supposedly similar dances, one performed by Candela alone and the other as a duet with José, you will find some differences, since in a solo dance, Candela does not have to wait or speed up her dance for anyone; she is on her own.

The Teaching Choreography

As language teachers, it is expected that we have planned our lessons, prepared our presentations, and created some class activities to keep our students busy and engaged in the classroom. It seems that everything is very well-rehearsed in advance. Of course, this is a good thing to do for all teachers. However, what we may forget is that our students are actually our dance partners in this duet without the benefit of having rehearsed with us. In fact, from the perspective of a language learner, every class meeting can feel like a forced dance without advance knowledge about the moves and choreography. For the most part, learners do not know what they will learn, how they will learn it, or what they are supposed to do with it. The teacher typically leads the dance, and the learners usually have to blindly follow. The teacher seldom coordinates with the students' moves.

I am sure most language teachers would like to coordinate their teaching with their students, but they wonder how this is even possible. The good news is that, unlike dance moves, class coordination has less to do with prior rehearsals and more to do with live engagement. Rather than a football coach practicing over and over with the players for an upcoming game, the classroom interaction can be more like two friends chatting about the topics they like to talk about with one another. The friends may not have agreed in advance about the topic when they meet, but because they already know something about each other's interest and way of talking, they do not really need to settle on a specific topic; they let that emerge. But I understand that this may seem a bit vague, especially in the context of teaching a second language. So, let me break down this concept into more concrete parts, especially as they relate to a language classroom.

Coordination

The most entertaining thing for my dog is the catch-a-rope game. She loves to run around the table trying to catch a rope while I try to make it harder for her to achieve her goal. But dogs are very clever creatures. I have noticed that even a 3-month-old puppy can come up with many strategies to achieve her goal. Without much effort, she can avoid obstacles such as my body and the table, adjust her speed and direction based on my movements, and even anticipate the future location of the rope while I am moving it in a certain direction. And all of these is done in real time and in a three-dimensional space.

When we think about learning, we can't help but think about conscious reflection on what we hear, see, or read. However, on a daily basis most of our actions are automatic and unconscious. It is impossible to think about the details of how to fry an egg for breakfast, how to put on our shoes, and where our feet and hands should be every second when driving to work. For the most part, we function on auto-pilot. Conscious thinking kicks in when automatic behavior fails to achieve its goals. The same is also true when we interact with others, such as our siblings, parents, colleagues, and friends. We learn how to coordinate our actions and discussions with them without even noticing it at the conscious level. Conscious behavior is tiring and takes a lot of effort to maintain. Similar to all species, we know that once we have learned something that works in our favor, we just let it happen without much thinking.

When language learners arrive at a class for the first time, they have already acquired a lot of automatic behavior suitable for a classroom learning/teaching environment. They know where to sit, when to talk, how to ask a question, and what to do when the teacher is talking or writing. They have learned all these actions from their prior classroom experiences and do all that very automatically. It is only when some of these automatic behaviors are not followed up properly that the teacher prompts a student by saying, "John, are you paying attention to what I am saying," or, "Can you please take notes. This is very important."

While it seems that students are forced to coordinate their moves with their teacher in a language classroom, there are many things a language teacher can do to facilitate a better choreography and anticipate unexpected moves. Here is a list of things that can help teachers coordinate with their learners and facilitate a better classroom interaction.

Tell and Show

If we have been using certain methods of teaching for a long time, it does not mean that our students also know that. Maybe their previous teacher had a different pedagogical approach. We should explicitly lay out the type of learning activities and assignments required from our students, especially what they need to do alone, for the teacher, and in group activities. We should tell them what kind of language materials and contents will be used in and out of the classroom and what students need do with them. Students should know and practice a typical day of class, broken down in time and tasks. After that, most class interactions become routinized. From then on, students will not have to worry about how to do something but rather concentrate only on what to do.

Body Talks

Most students do not talk unless we call on them. Even when they talk, it is usually very short and limited in scope. This lack of communication is even more noticeable in language classrooms. Language learners are generally very uncomfortable speaking in class in a new language. They are rightly afraid of being unable to express themselves correctly among peers. They would rather sit quietly than expose their grammatical and pronunciation errors. But for language teachers, knowing what student do not know can be as much important as what they know. Confused or uninterested faces, frowning, looking at other students for clues, and going back and forth between their books, the whiteboard, and the teacher are all signs. These non-verbal communication devices indicate something. Part of being a good dance partner in the language classroom is to know when to pause, speed up, stop, give a break, change the activity, repeat concepts, give more examples, or switch to another modality.

The body language is bidirectional. Learners, especially language learners, pay a lot of attention to the body language of their teachers. They try very hard to compensate for whatever they do not understand from the spoken words by paying attention to the way their teachers use hands, gestures, and body movements[1]. It is very important for language teachers to use their bodies to speak. Except for small cultural differences, body language is a universal language. We have to use it to our advantage. The good news is that a lot of these concerted efforts between teachers and language learners are recursive and build up quickly. Once we feel comfortable with the use of our body to communicate with others, we usually retain it and act on it very automatically.

Jury Rigging Language

One of my favorite phrases in English is the expression of 'jury rigging,' or sometimes also written as 'jerry rigging. This expression refers to crude actions of building or repairing something out of what people might have at their disposal rather than what must be used for a specific task. If your bathroom facet leaks on a Sunday evening and you can't call a plumber to come and fix it, you might 'jury rig' the leak with whatever material you might find in your household toolbox. Jurry rigging is a great way to know how things can work. It can also give us a different perspective to think about a problem. Jury rigging is the artistic way of being a plumber, electrician, car technician, and yes, even a language teacher. One way of jury-rigging language teaching is to make up our own teaching materials.

Make up Your Own Grammar

A lot of us think about grammar as laws of a language, governing what a language can and cannot do, in a way we think about the physical laws, such as the law of conservation of energy, famously introduced by Albert Einstein in $E = mc^2$. However, grammar is not the law of language. Grammar is just a convention, only one way of looking at the structure of a natural language. In fact, one of the most important contribution of Noam Chomsky to the field of linguistics was the idea that what we call grammar is only a surface-level organization of a language. He showed that if we look at the structure of a language not at the level of single words but as phrases that are allowed to move in certain ways, we would find another much deeper syntactical structure common among all languages[2].

Linguists, such as Noam Chomsky, intend to make sense of languages. They have found that certain forms of language have similar functions, and they labeled those forms into nouns, adjectives, adverbs, etc. For instance, it is assumed that the function of certain forms we call adjectives is to modify nouns. But the truth is that it is not only adjectives that modify nouns; nouns can also modify other nouns. 'Application' in 'application form' is a noun modifying another noun, 'form.' Similarly, adverbs do not modify only verbs; they also modify adjectives, as in 'very big ball,' and even modify other adverbs, as in 'so much trouble.'

The reverse is also true. That is, one function of language may be represented by different forms. For instance, we assume that in order to create a sense of future in English, we need to use either the form 'will,' as in 'I will walk,' or 'be going to,' as in 'I am going to walk.' However, the future tense can also be expressed using the simple present form, as in 'the bus leaves tomorrow morning at 12pm,' or the present progressive form, as in 'I am seeing a doctor tomorrow.'

It is important to know that every language learner can be potential linguist. He or she is trying to understand how the new language works. For the most part, we trust linguists to tell us just that. I think it is not a bad idea to start with an existing structure. However, we should not get bogged down to only one way. In fact, I will argue that the most efficient and permanent way of learning a new language is when learners come up with their own understanding how the new language functions. Let me explain.

When I was learning Spanish, I noticed that there are at least eight verbs that can replace the English verb, 'was.' It was initially very confusing to me to distinguish the different functions of 'estaba,' 'era,' 'fue,' 'fui,' 'había,' 'hubo,' 'estuve,' and 'fuera' that could replace one single verb in English. And this is only in the case of using 'was' for the first person singular. In English we only need two verbs, 'was' and 'were' for all cases referring to the number and persons in the simple past. In Spanish, all verbs are conjugated for all persons and numbers. So, there are at least 48 verbs in Spanish that can stand for 'was' and 'were' in English. Moreover, the same thing happens for many similar verbs in different tenses, such as 'is' for the present tense and many modals such as 'should,' 'would,' and 'could.'

Of course, there is no excessive use of verbs in Spanish; all different forms of verbs in Spanish relate to different functions that either do not exist in English or are collapsed into one. There are probably many ways to teach these differences to someone who lacks such features in their native language, such as English speakers. Most frequent way of teaching these differences is the typical grammar lesson. Each of these functions are related to a tense or mood and given a title, for example, *imperfect, past perfect, preterite,* and *anterior preterite*. Then, in the grammar lessons, teachers talk about *rules* of using these tenses in certain conditions. While a typical top-down grammar lesson has its uses, it has some major problems. For one, every time new language learners want to express an idea, first they must go through a mental list of rules to see which tense is needed to express that idea. Since most of our conversation is live and simultaneous, it becomes very cumbersome and taxing to constantly check for grammar accuracy while talking to another person. More importantly, it will take considerable amount of time to use the new language intuitively. We will have to constantly check our speech against a rule out there.

An intuitive way of learning the grammar of a language is to make the grammar for ourselves. We do not need to come up with clean and technical titles for tenses; all we need to do is to figure out how the use and function of a particular expression are related to certain forms in language, a bottom-up approach to learning a new language. In fact, this is the way children learn to speak their native language. No parent sits down with a child to discuss the parts of speech, the tenses, and the relative clauses. A parent just talks to a child and the child figures out how certain forms are used to achieve certain functions.

An adult is actually a lot more equipped to learn a new language through a bottom-up approach. A child cannot read and write; however, most adult can. For the most part, a child only needs to use language for basic and immediate physical needs. An adult, however, can express abstract ideas using complex form of language which allows for a much deeper understanding of the relationship between the form and function in a second language. While a child, through practice, may guess that words such as 'go,' 'sit,' and 'eat,' are used to tell a person to do something, what we would label as 'imperatives,' and adult can read passages in a book and pause to find out how sentences with 'have gone,' 'have sat,' and 'have eaten,' are used differently with that of 'went,' 'sat,' and 'ate.'

When we come up with our own understanding of how the new language works, we are in fact "jury-rigging" the language. It may take us longer time to achieve our goal, but we will have a much more intuitive sense about the new language, and we will have fun doing it. Jury rigging language is like assembling a castle with Lego parts or solving a crime while reading a mystery novel or checking the connection of the wires in a stalled car. Of course, we can always buy a ready-made toy castle or read the mystery novel to the end to find out the killer or to call the mechanic to fix the problem with the stalled car. But similar to learning the grammar of a new language, in all these instances we are just using things without ever knowing what they are made of and how they work. Once more, I am not trying to convince anyone that learning or teaching grammar is useless. Not at all. I only suggest that at the minimum we can also try to come up with our own understanding of language in parallel to relying on ready-made grammar lessons. In fact, these two can be very good complementary learning tools.

Some Practical Advice

You may now want to know how you can actually deconstruct a language and construct it for teaching, with a bottom up approach. The following is only a sample of ways you can approach this task. But I am sure, once you get your feet wet in that lake, very soon you will start swimming on your own.
As we discussed in the previous chapter, a lot of things in language education starts with meaningful content. I would advise to find level-appropriate, rich, and fun content. A short story, a new scientific finding, a podcast, an instructional YouTube video, a poem, a documentary, a story about a local event are all some good examples. It is best if the content is around one single theme. For most levels, it needs to be short enough to learn everything about it in a week or so and long enough that you can extract a few structures and some new words from it. If you or your students are very much interested in a particular book, you can also break down a book into a chapter a week.

Working out Words

Read or listen to the content once or twice. It is best to transcribe audio or video contents. First, concentrate only on important words. 'Important' in this case does not necessarily mean big words or advanced vocabulary. For the most part, it means words that are related to the same topic. Rather than concentrating on few big words, learners need to find the relationship between language items. In an article about a new space mission, words such as 'launch,' 'rocket,' 'engineers,' 'countdown,' 'orbit,' 'exploration,' 'Boeing,' 'reentry,' 'assembly,' 'valves,' and 'crew' should be made more prominent than other words. Of course, there will be more troubling words in the same content that have to be looked up to understand the content, and that is ok. Additionally, there will be many selected words that the learner is already somewhat familiar with. We are not interested in drilling the meaning of a word into the learner's brain but rather to allow the learners to come up with their own understanding of what a word could possibly mean in relation to other words in a particular context. As a teacher, we can then come up with our own activities with the selected words. Learners can summarize the report or give a one-minute oral impromptu speech implementing and using those words.

Working out the Structures

Read or listen to the content once or twice again, this time focusing on the structure used in the piece. 'Structure,' in this case, is not limited to classical grammatical features. In other words, it is important that a structure is extracted from the content itself and not superimposed to it. We do not want to fit our own assumptions about an English tense called the *present perfect* onto the content. Rather, we should highlight the instances that have particular forms in the content and discover their individual or collective functions.

Imagine your students are interested in the famous song by the group U2, *"I Still Haven't Found What I'm Looking For."* By looking at the lyrics of this song (please look it up), you will find out that there is a repeating structure consisting of 'have' plus a verb in a particular form. We can point out this feature, digest it, and discuss it. Does it always have to be 'have'? Can it be something different, for instance, 'has?' When? Why "I still haven't found" and not "why I did not have found?" Why do the verbs 'climb' and 'crawl' turn to 'climbed' and 'crawled' but 'run' and 'find' do not change to 'runed' and 'finded,' but instead to 'run' and 'found?' When we are done with the with the form, we can start asking questions about the function. What would be different if instead of, "I have climbed" and "I have scaled," the singer would have said, "I climbed' and "I scaled?" What would change in the meaning and how? Of course, there are many other features in the same song, for instance, why is it 'the fields' but 'these city walls?' What is the difference between 'the' and 'these?' Or, we can discuss the use of 'but' and 'still.' However, these are not the most salient features.

Other Features

Needless to say, we can do the same thing with many other aspects of language. These may include:

1. **Modality: spoken vs. written forms of language**

Example: What features of language change between a conversation among friends and a newspaper article?
Practice: Read a short news article, and then work with a partner to tell them in conversational style what happened. Then write a more academic summary of the same article.

2. **Phonetic: pronunciation, stress, tone, etc.**

Example: how do speakers make us pay attention to different

aspect of their talk by placing stress in different words
Practice: change the stress and intonation in a short talk and determine what stands out.

3. Discourse: formality/informality, poetry vs. prose, argumentation, expression of emotion, teasing, sarcasm, compliments, complaints, apologizing

Example: how modesty and humbleness are expressed in a short conversation from YouTube?
Practice: find out the adjectives, tone of talk, and discursive strategy that allows a speaker to show humbleness in a conversation between a young person and a respected scholar in the target culture.

CHAPTER 10

Conclusion

The Arts of the Sciences

There is a joke about a simple guy from a small town who arrives in a big city. Suffering from a headache from all the noise, traffic congestion, and pollution, he asks for a remedy. A city-dweller recommends taking an aspirin. Baffled, since he has never heard of the word, he asks, "What is an aspirin?" The city person shows him a little white pill and says, "This is an aspirin. You take it and it will cure your headache." In all sincerity, the small-town person responds, "Wow, that's a smart pill. How does it know that I have a headache and not a stomachache, or a toothache?" We may laugh at the simplicity of such a response. An aspirin does not need to know that we have a headache, and it does not have to. Aspirin works for any pain, for any part of the body, and for anyone living anywhere in the world. And most of us will take an aspirin for pain any day over any other alternatives offered to us.

Taking an aspirin to get rid of a common problem is not unique. We usually seek aspirin-like solutions for all our problems. We all want a near 100% accuracy and efficiency for solutions to any given problem without all the fuss of thinking about the other 'if' scenarios. A particular herbal tea may work for a particular headache and for some particular persons in a particular age group. However, seldom will an herbal tea or any other alternative medicine replaces the near accuracy of curing a headache like modern medicine, such as aspirin. Science offers near-universal solutions without 'ifs' and 'buts.' However, that universality for solving problems comes at a cost that we can usually afford to ignore. Per the above joke, an aspirin, for instance, does not get rid of a headache; it just lowers our threshold for sensing pain, no matter where it is or who takes it. And we do not care if the cure for our headache comes at the expense of losing a bit of sensation in all parts of our body. It works, so we take it. Aspirin works at the least common biological denominator, so it includes all bodies and all pains.

But hypothetically, what if you had the leisure of having a pharmacist who could create a very particular medicine for you to treat the ache of your head, not your tooth. I know it is a farfetched idea, but wouldn't you take it instead of an aspirin? In a way, we let science take care of all of *our* issues, so we do not have to think about *my* issues. If it works for someone else and it works for anyone else, it must work for me. But how far down are we willing to go to be treated similarly to everyone else for any of our issues? How far down are we willing to go to meet the minimum requirements for the common denominator that treats me like everybody else, with similar sensation, perception, pain, joy, comfort, sadness, and memory? For a headache, most of us do not have the luxury of a personal pharmacist. So, yes, we will go down to that common biological denominator. Yes, we will take an aspirin. We will numb down the whole body to get rid of a headache.

But what if someone told you that there is a book approved by scientists to teach anyone a new language in the most efficient way. Well, as an applied linguist, when I hear that statement, the first thing that jumps to my mind is that if that book is good for everyone, anywhere in the world, then by definition it cannot be the best book for everyone, everywhere. That is, if it is a *good* book for everyone, it cannot be the *best* book for an individual language learner. If you want the best book for you, then you do not need a scientist; you need an artist. In other words, science says what is good for everyone, and art says what is best for a person. Of course, there is a whole spectrum in between; nothing is black and white. For different reasons, mostly for practicality, we choose to take the route of universality, the science way. However, if we have the opportunity, of course, we prefer things to be custom-made for us, the artist way. Or do we?

The Artist Way of Teaching a Second Language

Throughout this book, I intended to show that there are fundamental differences in theory, approach, and method used between a scientist and an artist in teaching a new language. But I hope I was clear about a very important point: this difference is not so much about using distinct strategies or advantages of one approach over another. The difference is more about the perception we all have about the nature of learning a second language.

From a scientific perspective, learners are receivers. They need to be motivated with the right rewards, fed with the appropriate learning content, and offered adequate methods of learning. The goal is to get all these right: the right motivation, the right content, and the right approach. In the artist's way, however, there is an interaction between the learners and learning. These are never separated. This is a very counter-intuitive notion for most of us. We can understand how a book can change us. But it is extremely difficult to imagine that by reading a book we are also changing the book. Yes, by reading a book, that book is never the same book again, at least not to the person who read it. And such interactivity applies to all aspects of learning a second language, why learners want to learn a new language, what content may be more useful, and what method is most effective for them. We are constantly creating and recreating the learning itself. The artist's way of learning a new language, as such, is not about an attempt to create a custom-made aspirin pill for one's headache. It is about the notion that learners are more than passive recipient of a phenomenon called learning a second language. Learners are engaged in a unique and dynamic learning experience, and they can actively participate in shaping and reshaping such experience. The learning feeds them and they also feed the language. A new language is a living thing, a newborn baby of some sort. Babies must act like babies, but by acting like babies, they also require their parents to be more protective of them. Over time, they adjust their interactions; teenagers will act like teenagers, and the parents will have to give them more freedom. The same happens between language learners and the language they are learning.

Language as an Artistic Tool

What is the fastest way to learn a language? Which language program is the best in the country? How can I learn a new language like a child? How long does it take to learn a new language? What makes it difficult to learn a new language? What are some hacks to learn a new language? Is it too late to learn a new language if I am 35 years old? What is the best language learning app? How do you stay motivated when learning a new language? How many words do I need to know to be fluent in a new language? How do I learn Chinese in 3 months? Which language should I learn first? Can I learn a new language all by myself? These are some very typical questions that language educators receive from new language learners. But I feel that all these questions start with a wrong assumption. The assumption is that a language is something learners picks along the way as a side project that will stay in a part of their brain, until they call it up when needed. A lot of language learners treat a second language as another thing they can live without, but it does not hurt to have it. It is as though asking what if I already have a main home (first language), but just in case, how do I acquire a beach house (the second language)?

A guitar for Jimi Hendrix was not an add-on feature, as, "I already have a TV, let's get a guitar." Yes, it was a tool, but a tool that had rather become an extension of his arms and hands. Similarly, a paintbrush was not an add-on possession for Leonardo da Vinci. When a skilled painter is at work, you cannot point to a place where a paintbrush ends and the fingers of the painter starts; in the action of creating a painting, they are essentially one unit. The same is true for all those people who are good at what they do using tools. You cannot separate a chef, a carpenter, hairdresser, gardener, plumber, auto mechanic, dentist, and locksmith from their favorite tools. By the time people get to be very good at what they do, the tools they use have become an extension of their bodies. And you can see frequently that those people have respect for their tools. A new language functions in the same way. It is a living tool, but by the time we get to use it very well, it has become part of our body, and we must develop a certain respect for it.

The Art of Motivation

I have noticed that people accept cats as pets in three ways. There is the *indoor cat*, the *outdoor cat*, and then the *free-range cat*. The indoor cats are always at home and frightened to get out. Their owners feed them with care to make sure they have all the necessary nutrients and vitamins. They get their regular checkups from a veterinarian and might be even treated with occasional kitty care bubble spa. They have tons of toys to play with and owners who talk to them and treat them as a family member. The owners of the indoor cats quickly learn a lot about their cats, their food preferences, toys, and even moods. The indoor cats bring lots of joy to the home they live in, and the owners take pride in taking care of them. The owners of indoor cats get sad and sometimes even depressed when an indoor cat dies.

The outdoor cats, however, come and go in and out of the house as they wish. They have certain inter-dependencies accepted by both the cats and the owners. They enjoy their freedom of going to other places, but they usually come back home for plain cat food and a secure place for a night's sleep. They may get a vet visit occasionally but only if they suffer from a serious disease. They do not get to have a kitty spa, and the only toys they have might come from a garage sale. Both the outdoor cats and their owners are somewhat happy with this non-committal relationship. They want each other for minimal comfort, and they do not spend time getting to know one another at a deeper level. The owner is not concerned about the food and toy preferences of the outdoor cat, and the cat only wants the owner for the food, shelter, and occasional comfort. The owners of an outdoor cat get a bit sad when one dies, but very quickly they get over their sadness.

Finally, everyone knows the free-range cat. It belongs to everyone and no one. Everyone feeds it a bit, but no one takes it to the vet or buys it a toy. You never expect it to be around when you need one to pet, but while walking on the sidewalk you may get occasional joy pointing it to your daughter, "Oh, look, Fluffy is chasing a bird." In fact, 'Fluffy' has many names, as many as neighbors in the neighborhood. Nobody knows much about the free-range cat, and the cat knows even less about the neighbors. It takes a while for people to notice that a free-range cat has died, and they all share a bit of sadness when they don't find him around anymore. "Oh, I think Fluffy is gone. I hope he is in a better place," a neighbor might say to his daughter after noticing the cat's absence for quite some time.

The truth is that learners do not learn a language; they adopt one, like a living thing. So, similarly, there are three ways people adopt a language; they are called, *my-language*, *your-language*, and *their-language* people. The my-language people want to adopt a language in a mutually respectful and committed relationship. They understand that if I want the language to give me something, I will have to take care of it as well. The new language does not ask for a lot, but it wants us to know where it comes from, what it has been doing before us, and what it can do with us. More importantly, we have to be the proud owner of the new language and show it to others. The my-language people recognize that they are not just speaking a language but basking in the glory of thousands of years of culture, history, and literature.

As immigrants, such as myself, when we arrive in a new country, we benefit from the infrastructure, like roads, bridges, ports, shops, highways, public transportation, hospitals, universities, museums, galleries, airports, and so on, that generations of people have worked and paid taxes to build. We are using all that without having worked or paid for it. The least we can do is to show gratitude and willingness to contribute back. The same happens with learning a new language for my-language people. It only becomes my-language when I recognize that I am inheriting a semi-living entity, called language, that generations of ordinary people, writers, historians, poets, statesmen have lived their lives through it and with it. The least I can do is to be a proud speaker of the language and contribute back to it.

So, yes, we can safely adopt a new language as an outdoor cat (your-language) or a free-range cat (their-language), with minimum or no commitment at all. But we should not complain if we do not learn it fast enough or deeply enough. We were the ones who were not in a serious relationship with the language in the first place. We were the ones who wanted the new language because it only allowed us to talk to someone, my significant other for instance. But the new language for us always remained your-language, and never ours. We can even adopt a new language at a bare minimum of their-language when we need it to meet with our overseas business partners. If the jack in the trunk of my car is not working well and I get a flat tire on the road, I may use any big rock to hold the car elevated to change to an emergency tire. I may even carry the rock in the trunk for some time, but it will never replace my jack. So, I will get rid of it as soon as I do not need it anymore. Sometimes we treat languages as rocks to change a flat tire: when we have to use something but do not really want to. And of course, it is very heavy to haul it around, so we get rid of it when no longer needed.

Final Words

Let us end from where we started. The word *mercury* does not have a meaning. It acquires its meaning from the interaction between people and their history. If I am in an upscale restaurant in Santiago, Chile, and I am asked "El Mercurio?" from a waiter, it means that I am being asked if I subscribe to the Chilean newspaper, El Mercurio, so they can apply the discount to my bill. But such an incident is not limited to that particular word and that particular place. This process happens to all words. In fact, language learners truly learn the meaning of a word when they have learned its use in a given context. When learners are learning a new language, they use their native language as a base to figure out the meaning of the new words, the function of the new grammatical structures, and the sound system for the new language. They probe the new language with guesses in different instances and places and keep refining their understanding and performance. At some point the meaning, the sounds, and the function of words and sentences are no longer like definitions in the mind; they carry real experiences. And those experiences have not been inserted into their minds; they created them by interacting with the new language. It is only then that they can say they have learned the new language.

Index

A

abacus 25
acceleration 19, 20, 27
accent 36, 48, 50
  accents 36
accumulation 40, 75
achievement 68, 74
acquiring 50
acquisition 8, 15, 21, 38, 41, 43, 57, 64, 65, 66, 82, 90, 92, 104
acronyms 96
adulthood 49, 75
advocacy 52
aesthetics 16
affirmative 19
agency 26
algebra 65
  pre-algebra 58
alien 24
alphabet 75
American 27
  Latin American 37
  French-American 73
  Native American 28
analogy 70
anatomy 24
anterior preterite 120
anthropologist 41
apologizing 125
a posteriori 18
apparatus 41
applied linguistics 17, 63
appraisal 69
arbitrary 42
argumentation 125
articulation 49
artifact 23, 46, 85, 103
  artifacts 21
artisan 85, 86
artistic 10, 16, 20, 46, 49, 58, 65, 86, 87, 88, 91, 103, 118
aspiration 76
Aspirin 126, 127, 129
assembly line 84, 85
associative references 91
attention 8, 40, 43, 57, 73, 83, 104, 105, 108, 114, 116, 118, 124
attraction 72, 73, 98
auditory 31
Australian 27
authentic 98, 101, 102, 103
autonomic nervous system 69
auto-pilot 116
auxiliary verb 14, 19
Azeri Turkish 35

B

bachelor's degree 53
Balochis 35
ban on high-capacity magazine 52
Gregory Bateson 39, 41
Beethoven 22
bidirectional 118
black hole 44
blogs 82, 109, 110
David Bohm 15
bottom-up 121
Brexit 52
business presentation 87

C

Calligraphy 85
Cartesian 26, 29
Cencosud 13
certification 54
chaotic 17, 55
Chinese 47, 76, 85, 101, 102
Noam Chomsky 119
Chopin 72
choreography 114, 115, 117
classifications 16
climate change 52
cognitive 41, 63
Harry Collins 31
Christopher Columbus 55
Comic strips 110
coming-togetherness 40
common denominator 127
common ground 18

competency 53, 79, 82
complementary 122
comprehension 104
comprehensive 77
conscious 40, 59, 116
  consciously 104
  subconscious 68
context 3, 4, 5, 25, 28, 30, 52, 72, 87, 123, 133
  contexts 5, 43
controlled substances act 52
convention 119
  conventions 19, 54
coordinate 42, 114, 115, 116, 117
  coordinated 43, 114
  coordinates 60, 115
  coordination 93, 115
counter-intuitive 128
crocheting 56
cross-stitching 56
cubism 72
curriculum 53, 54, 101
cyberneticist 41

D

Leonardo da Vinci 130
deconstruct 122
decriminalization of marijuana 52
deficiency 56
definite article 14
degree of separation 107
Gilles Deleuze 42
department of motor vehicle

52
depression 71
descriptive 6, 33
determiners 14
deterministic 29
  deterministically 17, 29
dialogue 107
dilemma 71, 99
discourse 32, 33, 37, 44
  discourse analysis 30
DNA 24, 25
Drenching Contents 105
Drug Enforcement Administration 52
dualistic 29
Marcel Duchamp 73
duet dance 114
Dushanbeh 54
DVD 81
dynamic 17, 19, 27, 48, 74, 129
  dynamic process 75
  dynamics 9
  dynamic systems 56, 88

E

Eastern culture 34
eBooks 96
ecology 40, 105
educator 76, 84
  educators 6, 10, 22, 28, 45, 47, 89, 93, 113, 129
effectiveness 100, 103
efficiency 127
Albert Einstein 119
El Amor Brujo 114

embodied 30
embroidery 56
emergent 26, 73
emojis 27
enchantment 73
encounter 85, 103
  encounters 108
endeavor 59, 75
  endeavors 78
Endocrine System 69
engagement 74, 115
environment 17, 21, 27, 30, 42, 55, 71, 96, 104, 116
epistemology 29
ethologists 17
exit card 83

F

Facebook 111
Federal government 52
feedback 64, 79, 83, 84, 88, 90, 92, 95, 104
fight or flight 69
fill-in-the-blank 8, 43, 54
fine-tuning 58
first amendment 52
flamenco 114
flashcards 96
fluency 48, 64
formality/informality 125
framework 54, 66
free-range cat 130
French 42, 73, 82, 85, 89, 102, 107, 108
Sigmund Freud 17

G

gardenness 98, 99, 103
generalization 15
German 34, 51
gestures 118
Gilakis 35
Goethe 49
GPS 54, 55
grand jury 52
Greek 34

H

Hafiz 113
John Haiman 27
hallmark 30
Jimi Hendrix 130
hermosa 91
heuristic 18
homunculus 26
Hopi 28
House of Representative 52
Hyperlinkibility 109
hypothesis 101
hypothetically 127

I

IKEA 111
infinitesimal 20
infographics 93
infrastructure 132
Instagram 111
instinctual behavior 17
Integrative 66
intelligence 64, 106, 107
Interactional Expertise 31
interactive 47, 48, 60, 74, 75, 96, 111
interconnectedness 69
interface 30, 105
interlocutor 37, 88
intersection 99
intrinsic 66, 67
intuition 49, 68
intuitive 29, 113, 121, 128
Iran 35, 36, 37
iteration 44

J

jargon 10, 35
Steve Jobs 25
joint attention 104
judicial system 52
Jumbo 11
Carl G. Jung 17
jury rigging 118, 121

K

Kaunas 101
knitting 56
Kurds 35

L

language fossilization 92
language socialization 30
LBGTQ 52
legislation 52
Lider 35
linguistic anthropology 30, 63
Linguistic Relativity Principle

28
linguistics 5, 17, 21, 63, 119
Lithuania 101
locomotion 25
Konrad Lorenz 17

M

marketing strategies 47
martial arts 67
Mary Poppins 99
mass production 85
Mass production 86
mechanistic 15, 18
milestones 48, 59, 65
mindset 84
mnemonic devices 96
Monet 71
motivation 62, 63, 64, 65, 66, 67, 68, 69, 70, 72, 73, 76, 77, 78, 128, 130
multisensory 104
mutual gaze 104
my-language 131
Myspace 27
mystical 26
myths 28

N

native language 28, 29, 53, 56, 120, 121, 133
nervous system 21, 41, 58, 69, 70, 71, 89
nesting 16
networking 16
neuroscience 42, 63, 91

neurotransmitter 71
Isaac Newton 15
non-linear 106
non-verbal communication 118

O

object-oriented 16
obstacles 57, 68, 116
olfactory 31
overarching 87
overlap 34, 37, 93

P

paradox 55
Paris 54, 55
participate 79, 129
pathway 91
patterns 16, 20, 43, 44, 49, 50
Ivan Pavlov 17
pedagogical 19, 117
pen-pal 22
perception 7, 25, 26, 29, 31, 32, 42, 44, 89, 100, 127, 128
Persian 35, 36, 37, 51, 82, 85
phenomena 70, 71
phenomenon 21, 26, 129
philosophy 20, 29, 72
philosopher 42
philosophical 20, 28, 72
Phonetic 124
physiological 9, 69
physiologically 32, 106
Jean Piaget 89
Picasso 46, 71

Robert Pirsig's 20
podcast 109, 122
  podcasting 77
poetry 21, 97, 98, 125
pragmatic 93
pragmatics 22, 87, 90
predispositions 59
prescriptive 4, 10, 19
procedural memory 58
proficient 7, 41, 65, 69
pronunciation 7, 18, 22, 26, 27, 37, 48, 54, 87, 90, 92, 93, 95, 117, 124
Prozac 71
psychology 15, 17, 63
  psychological 71
  psychologist 89
  psychologists 17

Q

questionnaire 59, 76, 77, 93, 94

R

Rainer Maria Rilke 46
receptive skills 104
reciprocal 27
recursive 34, 37, 118
reductionism 15
reinforcement 83
relationship 20, 27, 28, 29, 31, 34, 36, 37, 39, 43, 44, 51, 52, 64, 72, 74, 75, 76, 101, 121, 123, 131, 132
repetition 44, 58, 91, 96
reward 64, 128
rewarding 69, 75
RNA 89
rudimentary 26
Rumi 72, 97, 99
Russian 82
RUT 12

S

Edward Sapir 28
John Schumann 69
self-esteem 68
semantic 22
semi-living organism 23, 27, 85
semiotics 63
serotonin 71
Shanghai 101
Theresa Shilhab 31
sobremesa 29
social media 82, 111
SSRI 71
statistics 17
stimulus 69, 91
  stimuli 69, 70, 89, 91
strategy 83, 99, 107, 125
  strategies 10, 47, 116, 128
structure 4, 5, 6, 7, 8, 9, 18, 20, 21, 22, 23, 25, 26, 29, 33, 34, 37, 42, 49, 88, 91, 93, 104, 119, 120, 122, 123, 124, 132, 133
  structural 18
subconscious 68
subjective 15, 16, 21, 66, 73, 103

symbolic 75, 90
syntactical 119
Systems Theory 41

T

Tajikistan 55
terminology 35
their-language 132
three-dimensional space 114
TikTok 22
Tolerance for Ambiguity 90
transcend 22
  transcendental 73
transformation 89
Turks 35
Twitter 27, 111

U

U2 123
UCLA 69
underlying 8, 70, 83
United Nations 52
utility 40, 78, 100

V

viewpoint 29, 30
vocabulary 11, 27, 32, 53, 54,
     84, 87, 90, 98, 102, 123

W

WhatsApp 27
Benjamin Lee Whorf 28
Ludwig Wittgenstein 31
Virginia Woolf 55

Y

your-language 132
YouTube 110, 122, 125

Z

Zeno's paradox 55

References

Chapter 1
1.
Taleb, Nassim N. "Antifragile: Things that Gain from Disorder." Vol. 3. Random House: New York, NY, 2012, p. 261.

Chapter 2
1.
Bohm, D. "Some Remarks on the Notion of Order." In Waddington, C. H. (ed.). Towards a Theoretical Biology. Sketches, Edinburgh Press: Edinburgh, 1969, pp. 18-40.
2.
Pirsig, Robert M. "Zen and the Art ofMotorcycle Maintenance." Bodley Head: London: , 1974.

Chpater 3
1.
Vygotsky, Lev S.. "Mind in Society: Development of Higher Psychological Processes." Harvard University Press: Cambridge, MA, 1978, p. 28.
2.
Whorf, Benjamin L. "Grammatical Categories. In Language, Thought,and Reality: Selected Writings of Benjamin Lee Whorf." John C. (ed.). MIT Press: Cambridge, MA: 1956 (1945), pp. 87–101.

3.
Churchland, Patricia S. "Neurophilosophy: Toward a Unified Science of the Mind-Brain." MIT press: Cambridge, MA, 1989.

4.
Varela, Francisco, Evan Thompson, and Eleanor Rosch. "The Embodied Mind." Vol. 10. MIT Press: Cambridge, MA, 1991.

5.
Schieffelin, Bambi B., and Elinor Ochs. "Language Socialization." Annual review of anthropology 15 (1986): pp.163-191.

6.
Schilhab, Theresa. "Derived Embodiment and Imaginative Capacities in Interactional Expertise." Phenomenology and the Cognitive Sciences 12.2 (2013): 309-325.

7.
Collins, Harry. "Language as a Repository of Tacit Knowledge." In Schilhab, T. and Stjernfelt, F. & Deacon, T. (ed.), The Symbolic Species Evolved, Springer: Dordrecht, 2012, pp. 235–239.

Chapter 4

1.
Bateson Gregory. "Mind and Nature. A Necessary Unity." Hampton Press: New York, NY, 1979, pp. 16-17.

2.
Bateson, Gregory. "The Cybernetics of 'Self': A Theory of Alcoholism." Psychiatry 34.1, 1971: pp. 1-18.

3.
Bateson, Gregory. "Form, Substance, and Difference. In Bateson, G. (ed.), Steps to an Scology of Mind. Ballantine: New York, NY, 1972.

4.
Deleuze, Gilles. "Difference and Repetition." Columbia University Press: New York, NY, p. 192.

Chapter 5

1.
Bateson, Gregory, and Bateson, Mary, C. "Angels Fear: Towards an Epistemology of the Sacred." Hampton Press: New York, NY, 1987, p. 28.

2.
Johnson, Addie. "Procedural Memory and Skill Acquisition." In Weiner, I. B. (ed.). Handbook of Psychology. Wiley: Hoboken, NJ, 2003, pp. 429-523.

Chapter 6

1.
Anjomshoa, Leila, and Firooz Sadighi. "The Importance of Motivation in Second Language Acquisition." International Journal on Studies in English Language and Literature (IJSELL) 3.2, 2015, pp. 126-137.

2.
Gardner, Robert C., and Lambert, Wallace E. "Motivational Variables in Second-Language acquisition." Canadian Journal of Psychology/Revue canadienne de psychologie 13.4, 1959, 266.

3.
Vallerand, Robert, J. "Toward a Hierarchical Model of Intrinsicand Extrinsic Motivation," in Advances in Experimental Social Psychology, M. Zanna (ed.), Academic Press: New York, NY, 1997, pp. 271-360.

4.
Gardner, Robert C., and Lambert, Wallace E. "Attitudes and Motivation in Second-Language Learning." Newbury House: Rowley, MA, 1972.

5.
Schumann, John H. "The Neurobiology of Affect in Language. A Supplement to." Language Learning, A Journal of Research in Language Studies 48,1997.

6.
Price, Lawrence H. "Serotonin Reuptake Inhibitors in Depression

and Anxiety: An Overview." Annals of Clinical Psychiatry 2.3, 1990: pp. 165-172.
7.
Camfield, William A. "Marcel Duchamp's Fountain: Its History and Aesthetics in the Context of 1917' in Dada/Surrealism, 1987, No. 16, pp. 69 – 70.

Chapter 7
1.
Hinkel, Eli. "Current Perspectives on Teaching the Four Skills." Tesol Quarterly 40.1, 2006, pp. 109-131.
2.
Taguchi, Naoko. "Second Language Acquisition and Pragmatics: An Overview." The Routledge Handbook of Second Language Acquisition and Pragmatics, Routledge: New York, NY. 2019, pp.1-14.
3.
Piaget, Jean. "The Role of Action in the Development of Thinking. In Knowledge and Development. Springer: Boston, MA, 1977. pp. 17-42.
4.
Ely, Christopher M. "Tolerance of Ambiguity and Use of Second Language Strategies." Foreign Language Annals 22.5, 1989, pp. 437-445.
5.
Selinker, Larry, and Lamendella, John, T. "Two Perspectives on Fossilization in Interlanguage Learning." Interlanguage Studies Bulletin, 3, 1978, pp. 143-191.

Chpater 8
1.
Goodwin, Charles. "Action and Embodiment within Situated Human Interaction." Journal of pragmatics 32.10, 2000, pp. 1489-1522.

2.
de Sousa, Alexandra, and Cunha, Eugénia. "Hominins and the Emergence of the Modern Human Brain." Progress in Brain Research 195, 2012, pp. 293-322.

Chapter 9
1.
Gullberg, Marianne. "Gestures and Second Language Acquisition." Handbook of Cognitive Linguistics and Second Language Acquisition. Routledge: London, 2008. pp. 286-315.
2.
Chomsky Noam. "Aspects of the Theory of Syntax." MIT Press: Cambridge, MA, 1965.